Healthcare Management Control

The COVID-19 pandemic has created unprecedented challenges for those responsible for the management of healthcare activities. These challenges require decision-makers at all levels to possess a broad and comprehensive understanding of healthcare management tools, and especially of the interaction between formal control systems and the informal power dynamics which operate within healthcare organisations. Managing in healthcare is not only difficult because of the sector's high-stakes ethical contexts but also because the healthcare workforce is inherently complex and heterogeneous.

It is the purpose of this book to survey the expanding literature on management control in healthcare with the aim of giving readers a better understanding of the options available to managers, decision-makers and also educated observers of this important sector. This book summarises key debates and findings in this rapidly developing and increasingly important field. It explores state-of-the-art models and approaches, highlights unexplored questions and gives an outlook on novel and developing trends.

In so doing it provides a hands-on guide for aspiring healthcare managers and practitioners and offers critical insights into the more advanced academic literature for those seeking a thorough grounding in the accounting and finance aspects of healthcare management.

Michelle Carr is Senior Lecturer in Management Control and Performance at University College Cork, Ireland.

Matthias Beck is Chair in Management and Vice Dean of Research at University College Cork, Ireland.

State of the Art in Business Research

Series Editor: Geoffrey Wood

Recent advances in theory, methods and applied knowledge (alongside structural changes in the global economic ecosystem) have presented researchers with challenges in seeking to stay abreast of their fields and navigate new scholarly terrains.

State of the Art in Business Research presents shortform books which provide an expert map to guide readers through new and rapidly evolving areas of research. Each title will provide an overview of the area, a guide to the key literature and theories and time-saving summaries of how theory interacts with practice.

As a collection, these books provide a library of theoretical and conceptual insights, and exposure to novel research tools and applied knowledge, that aid and facilitate in defining the state of the art, as a foundation stone for a new generation of research.

Complexity in Organizations
A Research Overview
Stig O. Johannessen

Organization Theory
A Research Overview
Gibson Burrell

Healthcare Management Control
A Research Overview
Michelle Carr and Matthias Beck

For more information about this series, please visit: www.routledge.com/State-of-the-Art-in-Business-Research/book-series/START

Healthcare Management Control

A Research Overview

Michelle Carr and Matthias Beck

Routledge
Taylor & Francis Group

LONDON AND NEW YORK

First published 2022
by Routledge
4 Park Square, Milton Park, Abingdon, Oxon OX14 4RN

and by Routledge
605 Third Avenue, New York, NY 10158

Routledge is an imprint of the Taylor & Francis Group, an informa business

British Library Cataloguing-in-Publication Data
A catalogue record for this book is available from the British Library

Library of Congress Cataloging-in-Publication Data
A catalog record has been requested for this book

ISBN: 978-0-367-69035-9 (hbk)
ISBN: 978-0-367-69036-6 (pbk)
ISBN: 978-1-003-14012-2 (ebk)

DOI: 10.4324/9781003140122

Typeset in Times New Roman
by Deanta Global Publishing Services, Chennai, India

Contents

1 Healthcare Management

Healthcare Management: An Introduction

The COVID-19 pandemic has created unprecedented challenges for those responsible for the management of healthcare activities. These challenges require decision-makers at all levels to possess a broad and comprehensive understanding of healthcare management tools, and especially of the interaction between formal control systems and the informal power dynamics which operate within healthcare organisations. Managing in healthcare is not only difficult because of the sector's high-stakes ethical contexts but also because the healthcare workforce is inherently complex and heterogeneous (Eldenburg, Krishnan & Krishnan, 2017).

Occupying a place at the top of the occupational hierarchy, clinicians exert considerable influence on how healthcare work is structured and organised (Malmmose, 2015). This can create tensions with those tasked with allocating resources within organisations as well as efforts to monitor or control outputs. Accounting research has looked into the socio-economic and political frameworks which facilitate or hinder the design and implementation of formal management control systems in the sector. Much of this work has centred on the healthcare sector where cost containment efforts or efforts to increase output have led to pressures to implement management control systems, often with the implicit objective of curtailing the power of medical professionals (Oppi, Campanale, Cinquini & Vagnoni, 2019). Today, management control systems are in place in most medium to large healthcare organisations, and at times an uneasy peace exists between those wanting to maintain clinician dominance and those seeking to manage output and performance in healthcare organisations. Meanwhile, a number of recent contributions from various sub-fields have explicitly thought to structure management interventions in a way that facilitates collaboration among a broad range of clinicians, managers and healthcare workers (Brennan & Flynn, 2013).

DOI: 10.4324/9781003140122-1

It is the purpose of this book to survey the expanding literature on management control in healthcare with the aim of giving readers a better understanding of the options available to managers, decision-makers and also educated observers of this important sector. We present this material in six chapters, which move the reader from a general discussion of management controls to specific applications. The final chapter discusses trends arising from developments in ehealth.

The Nature and Importance of the Healthcare Sector

Healthcare ranks amongst the largest economic sectors in many countries, not just in times of crisis but during periods of relative calm and steady economic expansion. In the 1960s healthcare expenditure accounted on average for less than 4 per cent of GDP across OECD countries. By 2007 this had risen to 9.6 per cent, and 12 OECD countries spent more than 10 per cent on healthcare. Healthcare expenditure as a share of GDP has since stabilised or fallen (OECD, 2018) in response to measures aimed at ensuring fiscal sustainability. Such measures were particularly prominent during the global recession of 2007/2008. The recent COVID-19 crisis is likely to lead to renewed increase in healthcare expenditure both in the short run and in coming years when problems arising from the temporary suspension of 'regular' care will need to be addressed and demands will be made for societies to be better prepared for crises of this kind. Meanwhile, legislative requirements, advances in service provision (technology and pharmaceuticals), altered public expectations, population aging and changing disease patterns will continue to place significant pressures on the management of healthcare systems (Corbett, d'Angelo, Gangitano & Freeman, 2017).

The focus of many developed countries has been on management reform. A central element of this reform movement has been the pursuit of improved performance, and this has particular relevance to management control in healthcare centred on management control and budgeting (Adinolfi, 2014). The label New Public Management (NPM) has been used to encapsulate various types of changes in public management. Hood (1991), a seminal theorist on NPM, suggests that, while NPM has been a significant global trend in international public administration since the mid-1970s, its intellectual origins can be traced back to a much earlier period. Typifying NPM as a 'marriage of opposites,' Hood (1991, p. 45) characterises it as a synthesis between post-World War II 'new institutional economics' and 'business-like public sector managerialism.' Growing out of this synthesis has been one hard to dispute change which is a common feature of NPM reforms: a growth in the power and influence of managers and management control practices in the healthcare sector, which is often accompanied by an emphasis on accountability. Hood (1995, p. 94) asserts that

> accounting is a key element in this new conception of accountability since it reflects high trust in the market and private business methods, and low trust in public servants and professionals whose activities therefore need to be more closely costed and evaluated by accounting techniques.

The increased prominence of management control practices prompted Power and Laughlin (1992, p. 132) to issue a note of caution highlighting the potential for management control to 'subvert existing value systems and to redefine the world or social space which it enters.' In this regard, Pavolini et al. (2018) identify healthcare organisations as being at particular risk. Specific sources of complexity in this context are highlighted in the next section.

Management Control in Healthcare

Healthcare structures and functions are similar in most developed countries, but there are also some important national differences that have implications for management control practices. It is important to note that many of these differences have evolved from a long history of incremental policy decisions, influenced by economic and non-economic factors as well as by specific institutions, such as the Catholic hierarchy or the power of the medical profession in English- and German-speaking countries (Cardinaels & Soderstrom, 2013).

In its widest sense, management control comprises measures and systems through which an organisation ensures that its activities conform to plan and its objectives are achieved. Management control has three core components: a performance plan with objectives, a means for measuring outcomes and measures which can be taken to address deviations from those objectives. In broad terms, management control practices are designed to help an organisation adapt to its environment and to deliver the results desired by its stakeholders (Otley, 2016). An organisation that is 'in control' is likely to perform well in meeting its objectives, regardless of whether these objectives are to maximise shareholder returns, heal the sick or educate the young.

Merchant and Van der Stede (2011) categorise management controls into: (i) action controls, (ii) personnel controls and (iii) result controls. This typology is adopted to discuss the operation of management control practices in the context of healthcare organisations. Action controls relate to the observation of acts by individuals as they carry out their work. In healthcare, action controls include structural constraints, such as passwords that restrict access and editing rights to information sources to authorised personnel only. Additionally, pre-action reviews involve the scrutiny and approval of the action plans of individuals before they are permitted to undertake certain courses of action. Examples include the approval by management of a clinician's plans for the purchase of a new piece of medical equipment. Action accountability, then, involves defining which actions are acceptable and which unacceptable in order to reward acceptable actions and punish unacceptable ones. Examples of action accountability measures in healthcare include instruction manuals, quality standards and action plans for different activities.

Action controls have been found to be most appropriate where cause and effect relationships are well understood. They are sometimes appropriate where it is possible to reliably predict that certain specified procedures will produce certain desired outcomes. An examination of the operation of action controls in the context of healthcare, however, also suggests that this type of service provision can involve the operation of many complex processes of different types, ranging from administrative tasks and protocols to services provided to patients by clinicians such as assessment and treatment. Healthcare operating processes are often highly complex and dynamic, involving many interconnected elements that exert a mutual influence on each other. Uncertainty in cause and effect relationships occurs relatively frequently because it can be very difficult to predict with certainty what outcomes will result from particular actions. This may be due to incomplete knowledge concerning the input/output relations or the highly interdependent nature of work processes with multiple inputs, which makes it difficult to programme workflows. In this way, the role of action controls can also differ across different sub-units in the context of a healthcare organisation, with some areas being characterised by greater and others by lesser levels of certainty and control.

Merchant and Van der Stede (2011) define personnel controls as those that enable employees to perform well by building on their natural tendencies to control themselves. A fundamental issue in implementing personnel controls in healthcare is the conflict of interest between the different stakeholders involved in the management of a healthcare organisation. Glouberman and Mintzberg (2001) characterise the internal organisation of healthcare as comprising four different professional groups: clinicians, nurses, management and trustees. Building on this, Cardinaels and Soderstrom (2013) correctly suggest that each professional group evaluates a healthcare organisation's decisions from its own standpoint, and that the differing perspectives can result in conflict between groups. In considering the operation of management control practices, conflicts of interest between management and clinicians are particularly important. Eldenburg, Hermalin and Weisbach (2004) and Mintzberg (1997) indicate that fundamental divergence between the viewpoints of clinicians and management primarily occurs in relation to how resources should be deployed. Furthermore, clinicians who are classified as 'dominant professionals' are primarily orientated towards providing effective clinical care for individual patients, while the management groups are orientated towards the efficient and effective use of resources for all patient groups, as well as the overall needs of the healthcare system (Mintzberg, 1997). These conflicts of interests have implications for the operation of management control practices, which aim to control resource usage for the healthcare organisation as a whole (Chua & Preston, 1994). The conflict is also compounded by the fact that core healthcare operating processes depend on the expertise of clinicians, thus granting them a significant degree of autonomy. Furthermore, the training and education of clinicians have long emphasised their role in advocating for their patients, to ensure that they receive effective care. In order to be patient advocates, however, clinicians often believe that they must also maintain clinician autonomy to determine the care needed. The literature has given considerable attention to examining this issue, and we return to this topic again.

Result controls relate to the gathering and reporting of information concerning the outcomes of work efforts. Establishing such controls requires the selection of performance measures. However, the selection of performance measures can be a difficult and onerous task in healthcare contexts. While most private organisations have finance-related goals focused on maximising profits and satisfying stakeholders, healthcare organisations tend to adopt more broadly defined mission statements. For example, 'equity and fairness' are frequently stated principles of healthcare policy. However, such abstract objectives lack a clear focus and are difficult to measure. This creates a political environment where preferences in healthcare are continuously challenged and debated, which ultimately can translate into goal ambiguity at the micro-level of healthcare organisations themselves, as they attempt to respond to the political agenda through resource allocation decisions.

The operation of result controls also requires performance to be measured, but in healthcare reliable and precise measurement of performance is not always attainable. For example, 'quality of care' is an important healthcare outcome but it can again be difficult to measure and interpret. In addition, patient service outcomes (including care and cure of the patient) are, in contrast with other service products, intangible and cannot be packaged or stocked (Abernethy et al., 2006). As an emotive issue healthcare attracts considerable media attention. This focus makes the sector more visible to the public, and thereby may raise expectations regarding the quality and availability of services. Finally, the operation of output controls in healthcare is complicated by the fact that the organisational charters of these organisations typically preclude the use of monetary incentives as a mechanism for achieving goal congruence, thus making the implementation of any system of reward or punishment a very complicated task (Eldenburg et al., 2017).

In summary, conflicting goal sets and expectations as well as problems of output measurement and comparison make the implementation of management control practices in healthcare difficult, such that control mechanisms often come to play a symbolic or ritualistic role with which healthcare workers are reluctant to engage (Lunkes, Naranjo-Gil & Lopez-Valeiras, 2018). Research has proposed improvements to management control practices to win broader support from relevant healthcare stakeholders (Pizzini, 2006; Uyar & Kuzey, 2016).

Book Structure

This book summarises key debates and findings in this rapidly developing and increasingly important field. It explores state-of-the-art models and approaches, highlights unexplored questions and gives an outlook on novel and developing trends. In so doing we provide a hands-on guide for aspiring healthcare managers and practitioners and offer critical insights into the more advanced academic literature for those seeking a thorough grounding in the accounting and finance aspects of healthcare management. Chapter 2 locates the study within the domain of management control research. It provides a review of the management control literature, which will form the study framework (Harris, 2017). Chapter 3 provides a review of the extensive literature relating to control mechanisms as means of organisational improvement, focusing on key features of management control approaches and the diverse factors that affect their use. Factors such as the difficulty and specificity of budget targets, the participation of individuals in setting them and perceptions around the relevance and usefulness of management control information affect the efficacy of control measures (De Loo, Verstegen & Swagerman, 2011). Chapter 4 focuses on research exploring the use of, and problems associated with, budgetary control for healthcare users and stakeholders such as management and clinicians (Oppi et al., 2019).

Chapter 5 reviews the applicability of the contemporary management control practices to healthcare contexts (Naranjo-Gil, Sánchez-Expósito & Gómez-Ruiz, 2016). It has been suggested that budgetary control has lost relevance due to changing organisational environments (Rababah & Bataineh, 2016). In response a number of new management control practices, such as the balanced scorecard system, activity-based costing and benchmarking in healthcare settings have been developed. Considerable research has made important contributions to exploring the link between the operation of these new approaches and behavioural responses of healthcare staff with a view towards drawing lessons for managers. This chapter reviews this research.

Chapter 6 addresses some of the challenges which healthcare management is likely to face in the next decades such as changes in pharmaceuticals provision, new approaches to care and advances in medical technology some of which are linked to concepts of personalised medicine, eHealth, telehealth or virtual health. Studies on the managerial implications of eHealth-related changes are introduced as a basis for discussion of the factors that will affect the use of these developments. Questions are raised about the dissolution of traditional hierarchical structures as new roles in healthcare are created. Issues of trust required of both medical staff and the recipients of medical services are examined.

References

Abernethy, M. A. (1996). Physicians and resource management: The role of accounting and non-accounting controls. *Financial Accountability and Management*, *12*(2), 189–204.

Abernethy, M. A., Chua, W. F., Grafton, J., & Mahama, H. (2006). Accounting and control in health care: behavioural, organisational, sociological and critical perspectives. *Handbooks of management accounting research*, *2*, 805–829.

Adinolfi, P. (2014). Barriers to reforming healthcare: The Italian case. *Health Care Analysis*, *22*(1), 36–58.

Brennan, N. M., & Flynn, M. A. (2013). Differentiating clinical governance, clinical management and clinical practice. *Clinical Governance: An International Journal*, *18*(2), 114–131.

Cardinaels, E., & Soderstrom N. S. (2013). Managing in a complex world: Accounting and governance choices in healthcare. *European Accounting Review*, *22*(4), 647–684.

Chua, W. F., & Preston, A. (1994). Worrying about accounting in healthcare. *Accounting, Auditing and Accountability Journal*, *7*(3), 4–17.

Corbett, J., d'Angelo, C., Gangitano, L., & Freeman, J. (2017). *Future of health: Findings from a survey of stakeholders on the future of health and healthcare in England*. Cambridge: Europe.

De Loo, I., Verstegen, B., & Swagerman, D. (2011). Understanding the roles of management accountants. *European Business Review*, *3*(3), 287–313.

Eldenburg, L., Hermalin, B. E., Weisbach, M. S., & Wosinska, M. (2004). Governance, performance objectives and organizational form: evidence from hospitals. *Journal of Corporate Finance*, *10*(4), 527–548.

Eldenburg, L. G., Krishnan, H. A., & Krishnan, R. (2017). Management accounting and control in the hospital industry: A review. *Journal of Governmental and Nonprofit Accounting*, *6*(1), 52–91.

Glouberman, S., & Mintzberg, H. (2001). Managing the care of health and the cure of disease—Part I: Differentiation. *Health Care Management Review*, *26*(1), 56–69.

Harris, E. (2017). Introduction to performance management and control. In *The Routledge companion to performance management and control* (pp. 1–9). Routledge: New York.

Hood, C. (1991). A public management for all seasons. *Public Administration, 6*(3), 3–19.

Hood, C. (1995). The new public management in the 1980s: Variations on a theme. *Accounting Organisations and Society, 20*(2–3), 93–109.

Lunkes, R. J., Naranjo-Gil, D., & Lopez-Valeiras, E. (2018). Management control systems and clinical experience of managers in public hospitals. *International Journal of Environmental Research and Public Health, 15*(4), 776.

Malmmose, M. (2015). Management accounting versus medical profession discourse: Hegemony in a public health care debate—A case from Denmark. *Critical Perspectives on Accounting, 27*(1), 144–159.

Merchant, K., & Van der Stede, W. (2011). *Management control systems: Performance measurement, evaluation and incentives.* Harlow: Prentice Hall.

Mintzberg, H. (1997). Towards healthier healthcare. *Healthcare Management Review, 22*(4), 9–18.

Naranjo-Gil, D., Sánchez-Expósito, M. J., & Gómez-Ruiz, L. (2016). Traditional vs. Contemporary management control practices for developing public health policies. *International Journal of Environmental Research and Public Health, 13*(7), 713.

OECD (2014–2018). *Health at a Glance (various years).* OECD: Paris.

Oppi, C., Campanale, C., Cinquini, L., & Vagnoni, E. (2019). Clinicians and accounting: A systematic review and research directions. *Financial Accountability and Management, 35*(3), 290–312.

Otley, D. (2016). The contingency theory of management accounting and control: 1980–2014. *Management Accounting Research, 31*(3), 45–62.

Pavolini, E., Kuhlmann, E., Agartan, T. I., Burau, V., Mannion, R., & Speed, E. (2018). Healthcare governance, professions and populism: Is there a relationship? An explorative comparison of five European countries. *Health Policy, 122* (10), 1140–1148.

Pizzini, M. J. (2006). The relation between cost-system design, managers' evaluations of the relevance and usefulness of cost data, and financial performance: An empirical study of US healthcare. *Accounting, Organisations and Society, 31*(2), 179–210.

Power, M., & Laughlin, R. (1992). Critical theory and accounting. *Critical Management Studies, 21*(5), 441–465.

Rababah, A., & Bataineh, A. (2016). Factors influencing balanced scorecard implementation. *Research Journal of Finance and Accounting, 7*(2), 204–212.

Uyar, A., & Kuzey, C. (2016). Does management accounting mediate the relationship between cost system design and performance? *Advances in Accounting, 35*(4), 170–176.

2   Management Control Domain

Management Control Definitions

In broad terms, management control practices are designed to help an organisation adapt to its environment and to deliver the results desired by its stakeholders (Otley, Broadbent & Berry, 1995). An organisation that is 'in control' is likely to perform well in meeting its objectives, regardless of whether these objectives are to maximise shareholder returns, heal the sick or educate the young (Merchant & Van der Stede, 2011). Beyond this general understanding, however, definitions and classifications of management control vary widely. This section examines the most prevalent of these definitions and classifications.

The literature contains a large number of definitions of management control (Fisher, 1998). In the 1960s, Anthony (1965, p. 17) separated management control from both strategic planning and operational control and defined it as 'the process by which individuals ensure that resources are obtained and used effectively and efficiently in the accomplishment of the organisation's goals.' Effectiveness can be understood as achieving pre-defined objectives, while efficiency relates to the extent to which those objectives are achieved economically. Anthony's (1965) framework guided management control research and teaching for many decades and underpinned an emphasis on financial accounting-based management control practices. However, broader definitions of management control have emerged over the years as researchers have adopted different approaches to their study, drawing on other management disciplines as well as the social and behavioural sciences, cybernetics and the humanities. Simons (1987, p. 5) defines management control as 'the formal, information-based routines and procedures individuals use to maintain or alter patterns in organisational activities.' Following this example, some researchers have outlined very broad conceptions of management control. Thus, Chenhall (2003, p. 129) describes management accounting as a 'collection of practices such

DOI: 10.4324/9781003140122-2

as budgeting or product costing,' and management accounting systems as the 'systematic use of management accounting to achieve some goal,' and management control systems as 'a broad term that encompasses management accounting systems and also other controls such as personnel and clan controls.' Merchant and Otley (2006, p. 785) similarly note that management control can include factors such as strategic development, strategic control and learning processes, and conclude that it is 'anything designed to help an organisation to adapt to the environment in which it is set and to deliver the key results desired by stakeholder groups' to 'keep organisations on track.'

One prominent group of researchers has focused on the behavioural implications of management control. For example, Flamholtz, Das and Tsui (1985, p. 36) describe management control as 'attempts by the organisation to increase the probability that individuals will behave in ways that lead to the attainment of organisational goals.' Meanwhile, Merchant and Van der Stede (2011, p. 8) characterise it as 'including all the devices or systems individuals use to ensure than the behaviours and decisions of their employees are consistent with the organisation's objectives and strategies.' This chimes with earlier works by Abernethy and Chua (1996, p. 573) who state that a management control system comprises 'a combination of control mechanisms designed and implemented by management to increase the probability that organisational actors will behave in ways consistent with the objectives of the dominant organisational coalition.'

In an effort to explore variations in the way management control has been defined, Malmi and Brown (2008, p. 290) proposed a definition of management control that includes 'all the devices and systems individuals use to ensure that the behaviours and decisions of their employees are consistent with the organisation's objectives and strategies.' This definition is echoed by Ferreira and Otley (2009, p. 267) who define management control as the

> evolving formal and informal mechanisms, processes, systems and networks used by organisations for conveying the key objectives and goals elicited by management, for assisting the strategic process and on-going management through analysis, planning, measurement, control, rewarding and broadly managing performance, and for supporting and facilitating organisational learning and change.

While definitions of management control have evolved towards a behavioural and strategic emphasis, the central question has remained the same: how can management control practices be developed to help ensure that an organisation achieves its objectives? For clarity this book uses the term 'management control practice' to describe devices that organisations use to ensure that individuals work to achieve the organisation's strategic objectives, while the term 'management control system' is used as suggested, by Merchant and Van der Stede (2011), to refer to the portfolio of management control practices that organisations can employ to this end. It is important to recognise that management control practices come in many different forms, from simple operating procedures to more elaborate performance evaluation processes. Researchers have categorised these management control practices in a variety of ways. The next section will discuss this work.

Management Control Typologies

The forms through which management control manifests itself in organisations have been classified in a variety of ways. For example, Hopwood (1974) categorised control as administrative controls, social controls and self-controls. Administrative controls denote the formal rules and standard procedures used to regulate the behaviour of individuals within the organisation. This type of management control focuses on the output resulting from behaviour and actions rather than the behaviour itself. In contrast, social controls develop informally to regulate individuals' behaviour. In other words, by establishing social relationships with colleagues, individuals may become socialised into accepting the dominant norms and values within the social network of their workplace. Finally, self-controls refer to those rules that are internalised so that individuals will typically behave according to a certain established norm. Writing a few years after Hopwood, Ouchi (1979) categorises management controls into behavioural controls and output controls. Behavioural controls refer to personnel surveillance and direct supervision that monitors individuals' activities. Output controls, then, denotes the monitoring of output results so that they are recorded in written form. In his study of a supply division, Ouchi (1980) identifies three types of management control mechanisms: market mechanisms, bureaucratic mechanisms and clan mechanisms. Market mechanisms provide control in so far as they measure and reward individual contributions. Bureaucratic mechanisms rely upon a mixture of close evaluation with a socialised acceptance of a common objective. For Ouchi (1980), clan mechanisms rely upon socialisation processes that effectively eliminate goal incongruence between individuals and the organisation they work for.

Macintosh (1994) categorises management controls into five categories: bureaucratic, charismatic, market, tradition and collegial controls. Bureaucratic controls emphasise hierarchy, procedures, rules and record-keeping and are suitable to situations characterised by certainty and the absence of ambiguity. Conversely, charismatic controls are appropriate where objectives are unambiguous but the means by which they are to be achieved are uncertain. Typically, charismatic controls are associated with revolutionary change, and it has been suggested that a fundamental element of this type of control is the importance of a charismatic leader. Market controls are characterised as acting as the disciplinary glove on the invisible hand through the organisation's performance in the market. Control by tradition suggests that beliefs, rights and norms are handed down and generally followed in the interests of the greater good. Finally, collegial controls relate to specific groups possessing privileged authority (e.g. clinicians) where the administrators are themselves subject to this control.

Fisher (1995) distinguished between general management control practices and formal management control practices. General management control practices operate via standard operating procedures (SOPs), organisation structure, organisation culture and human resources policies. Formal management control practices are based on performance targets, observed results and feedback (i.e. a cybernetic model). According to Fisher (1995) general management control practices are not formal systems *per se*, but they do impact on the operation and effectiveness of formal management control practices. Fisher (1995) provides a useful list of macro control attributes that can be used to describe the general orientation of management control practices. A summary explanation of each attribute is detailed in Table 2.1.

Merchant (1985) and Merchant and Van der Stede (2011) distinguish between result, action, personnel and cultural controls. Result controls involve defining the output that individuals are expected to deliver to receive a reward or otherwise. Action controls evaluate the means taken to achieve the objective as opposed to the result in itself. In this way, action controls prohibit undesirable behaviour (as behavioural constraint), derive desired behaviour from plans (as pre-action review) and monitor behaviour directly by observation or via formal controls (as action accountability). Personnel controls are primarily constructed so that individuals will process a desired task satisfactorily on their own, for instance based on their training, in contrast to cultural controls which shape organisational norms. Cultural controls take into account recruitment, training and promotion of norms to reinforce individual self-control. This typology was used in Chapter 1 when we explored the operation of management control practices in the context of the healthcare sector.

This discussion of management control typologies highlights the broad range of management control practices that may be employed to ensure that management control is achieved. Moreover, as many of the classifications have strong similarities, different management control typologies are often discussed synonymously (Malmi & Brown, 2008). Consequently, management control frameworks have been developed to facilitate the study of management control practices. These will be examined in the following section.

Table 2.1 Attributes of Management Control Practices

Macro Control Attribute	Description
Tight versus loose	Degree of actual enforcement of a management control practice.
Objective versus subjective	Extent to which a management control practice is based on pre-determined formula and policies rather than on subjective evaluation.
Mechanistic versus organic	Extent to which a management control practice is applied methodically without consideration of contextual factors or exceptions.
Short-term versus long-term	Extent to which a management control practice is based on short-term or long-term performance measures.
Group versus individual	Extent to which a management control practice target is applicable to all sub-units within the organisation or tailor-made to each sub-unit.
Interactive versus programmed	Extent of involvement of evaluator in a management control process.
Administrative versus interpersonal	Administrative management control practice would imply greater emphasis on subordinate budget participation, rather than on achievement of budget targets and more detailed budget data.
Behaviour versus outcome	Extent to which a management control practice focuses on regulating behaviour (the means) rather than assessing results (the end) only.

Source: modified from Fisher (1995, p. 28).

Management Control Frameworks

Given the complexity of issues associated with the practice of management control, researchers have developed frameworks to better understand the core processes involved. In an early and influential effort to do so, Otley and Berry (1980) built on the discipline of cybernetics to describe the nature of controls. According to Otley and Berry (1980) four essential criteria must apply for a process to be deemed under control: (i) the system must have an objective; (ii) it must be possible to measure results in relation to that objective; (iii) the system must have a predictive model; and (iv) a number of alternative actions must be available for selection. Borrowing from cybernetics this model incorporates both feedback and feed-forward control. Feedback control involves detecting deviations or errors in actual outcomes, compared with planned outcomes, and instigating any required corrective action as a result, while feed-forward control involves detecting deviations or errors in predicted outcomes, compared with planned outcomes, and similarly implementing any corrective action deemed necessary to achieve the planned outcome (Otley & Berry, 1980).

Thus, feedback control is retrospective while feed-forward control is prospective in nature.

Otley and Berry (1980) argue that their framework contains the essential building blocks of a traditional management control system, that is, the setting of objectives, the preparation of budgets, performance measurement, feedback and feed-forward regulation mechanisms, the calculation of variances and the consideration of alternative courses of action. However, they also recognise the limitations of this framework which include: (i) objectives can be difficult to define or to reconcile between varying groups within an organisation; (ii) predictive management control practices are often imprecise and inaccurate and there are usually several alternative predictive control models within a given management control system; (iii) identifying an appropriate measure with which to compare actual results and desired objectives is a complex task and may lead to organisational conflict as it will not always be considered appropriate for such measures to be financial in nature; and (iv) for a control system to be effective individuals must be persuaded to implement the required actions. These challenges are indicative of an overarching problem in designing control practices, namely, individuals themselves can take on the form of self-controlling systems and, therefore, may react in ways that are difficult to predict. Despite these limitations, this framework represented a significant step forward in relation to the management control concepts proposed by Anthony (1965). Its main contribution consisted of the fact that it sought to facilitate a holistic approach to management control, which relates strategic objectives to day-to-day operational processes and continuously revisits each stage of the process as events develop.

Another framework that merits discussion is the *Levers of Control* framework developed by Simons (1987). This framework was inductively derived from case studies and related discussions with senior managers. According to Simons (1987), there are four key types of control, or levers, about which senior individuals must make explicit decisions regarding the relative appropriateness of each. The four types of control levers identified in the framework are belief systems, boundary systems, interactive controls and diagnostic controls. Belief systems set the core values and contribute to the overall culture and ethos of an organisation. They instil in an individual the central aspirations of an organisation in terms of the values it aspires to create. To achieve this, they may operate through devices such as mission statements and overall corporate policies. Boundary systems involve the setting of limits and rules which employees are discouraged from exceeding or infringing. Simons (1987) describes belief and boundary systems as the 'yin and yang' of organisational control. In his view, beliefs are warm, positive and inspirational in nature but are controlled by the dark, cold constraints of boundary systems. Diagnostic control is manifest in the processes of variance accounting or management by exception that are typically implemented by senior management to track the progress of individuals, departments or units by measuring their performance against pre-defined targets. In contrast, interactive control is used to distinguish strategic failure from inadequate strategic implementation. In this regard, interactive controls are intended to give early warnings that a given strategy is no longer appropriate to a given situation and hence needs revision.

Empirical research has tended to focus on the interactive and diagnostic elements of the Levers of Control framework and the use of specific management control practices. For example, Tuomela (2005) found that the 'Balanced Scorecard' (BSC) can be used in two ways: diagnostically and interactively. BSCs are a management control device aimed at translating multiple organisational gaols into measurable performance objectives. Notably, he concluded that context is very important, as his study found that resistance to change developed as new information made actions more visible, power structures shifted and workload increased. Similarly, using data from 63 public healthcare CEOs, Abernethy and Brownell (1999) found that budget control practices were used both diagnostically and interactively. Abernethy and Brownell's (1999) study also showed that an interactive style of budget use can mitigate the disruptive performance effects of the strategic change process. Subsequently, Henri (2006) compared the differing impact of using management control practices interactively and diagnostically. This study found that the diagnostic use of management controls had a negative effect on strategic capabilities (i.e. market orientation, entrepreneurship, innovativeness and organisational learning) and that interactive use had a positive effect. Bisbe and Otley (2004) examined the relationship between the interactive use of management control practices and innovation and found that the direction—positive or negative—of the relationship was contingent upon the level of innovation in the organisation. For high-innovation organisations, the interactive use of management control practices was negatively associated with innovation, while in low-innovation organisations the analysis suggested a positive direction of relationship. Research exploring the belief and boundary elements of the Levers of Control framework, see Collier (2005), found that informal controls such as group norms, socialisation and culture were more important than formal controls. Widener (2007) found evidence of interdependence and complementarity between all four levers of control and hence suggested that the full benefit of management control arises when they are used both diagnostically and interactively.

Empirical research has identified a number of strengths and weaknesses in relation to Simon's (1987) highly influential 'Levers of Control' framework. In terms of strengths, Langfield-Smith (2008, p. 220) asserts that the framework provides a complex conceptualisation of 'the use of management control practices to manage behaviour and effect strategic change.' Ferreira and Otley (2009) contend that the Levers of Control framework is useful in offering a broad perspective of management control by taking account of the range of controls employed and how they are used by various organisations. However, with regard to weaknesses, Collier (2005) maintains that, while Simon's framework attempts to include informal groups, the conceptualisation of belief systems does not encompass other informal controls such as group norms, socialisation and culture. A further limitation is that the framework is strongly focused on the top level of management and is difficult to translate to lower hierarchical levels (Ferreira & Otley, 2009).

Otley (1999) sought to ensure that a holistic view of management control practices was preserved beyond the Simon approach and, therefore, proposed his Performance Management framework. This framework was founded on the premise that good results are likely to be produced by many alternative management control system configurations and, hence, studying only one aspect of management control system design at a time will tend to introduce statistical noise into the results. For example, Otley (1999) argues that the light use of one control practice (e.g. budget control) may be counterbalanced by the heavy use of an alternative control practice (e.g. the Balanced Scorecard) and vice versa. Therefore, he suggests that it is only when the overall management control system is considered that meaningful connections between the use of management control practices and the overall results can emerge. The Performance Management framework is based around five central questions:

i. What are the key objectives that are central to the organisation's overall future success, and how can it evaluate its achievement of each of these objectives?

ii. What strategies and plans has the organisation adopted, what are the processes and activities that it will require to successfully implement these, and how will it assess and measure the performance of these activities?

iii. What level of performance does the organisation need to achieve in each of the areas defined in questions (i) and (ii), and how will it set appropriate performance targets for them?

iv. What rewards will individuals gain by achieving these performance targets or, conversely, what penalties will they suffer by failing to achieve them?

v. What are the information-flows (feedback and feed-forward loops) that are necessary to enable the organisation to learn from its experience, and to adapt its current behaviour in the light of that experience?

(Otley, 1999, p. 366)

Otley (1999) applies this framework in discussing three major management control practices —budget control, the Balanced Scorecard and economic value added—to demonstrate how each practice takes different approaches to each of the five main areas he identifies (see above). Researchers have highlighted a number of key strengths of the Performance Management framework. Stinger (2007) has commended the approach for the breadth of management control issues it encompasses and for its integrated nature. The framework is straightforward in its application, and the areas it addresses are considered meaningful at different levels of management (Ferreira & Otley, 2009). However, a number of weaknesses have also been highlighted. For instance, the Performance Management framework has been criticised for under-playing the roles of vision and mission in management control when compared to Simons' (1987) 'Levers of Control' framework. An additional criticism is that it fails to recognise the importance of management control use, despite the importance given to this factor in the literature (Hopwood, 1974; Otley, 1978; Simons, 1987). Finally, it has been noted that the interconnections between the different management control practices have not been explicitly addressed in the framework (Malmi & Granlund, 2009; Stringer, 2007).

In 2009, Ferreira and Otley proposed a further development to their performance management and control framework. Drawing on additional case study data, this framework sought to refine the insights of Otley (1999) and Simons (1987). The new framework expanded the original 5 questions to 12, 8 of which related to the management of objectives and the means by which this would be achieved. The other four questions related to underlying issues that influence the operation of management control practices. Based on a range of findings in the literature, Ferreira and Otley (2009) propose that variables relating to external environment, strategy, culture, organisational structure, size, technology and ownership structure all influence the operation of a management control system. By including these factors, the framework is designed to provide a broad view of the key aspects of management control practices and to form the basis upon which further investigation can be developed (Ferreira & Otley, 2009). The 12 questions contained in Ferreira and Otley's (2009) framework are:

i. What is the organisation's vision and mission and how is it communicated internally? What mechanisms, processes, and networks are used to express the organisation's overarching strategy and objectives internally?

ii. What are the key factors that are believed to be fundamental to the organisation's long-term success and how are they communicated internally?

iii. What is the organisation hierarchy and how does it align with the design and use of the management control practices? How does it influence and how is it influenced by the control practice in situ?

iv. What goals and objectives has the organisation adopted, and what are the key success factors that will be used to decide if they are successful? How are goals and objectives adapted, generated and communicated?

v. What are the organisation's key control measures deriving from its goals, key success factors, objectives and plans? How are these quantified and connected, and what role do they play in performance evaluation?

vi. What level of performance does the organisation need to achieve in the key performance measures, and how does it approach target setting, in terms of difficulty and participation levels?

vii. What manner, if any, does the organisation follow for evaluating employee, sub-unit, and organisational performance? Are performance evaluations primarily objective, subjective or mixed, and how important are formal and informal information and controls in these processes?

viii. What rewards—extrinsic and/or intrinsic—will be awarded by achieving performance targets or other assessed aspects of performance (or equally, what penalties will be imposed by failure to achieve)?

ix. What specific information-flows (feedback and feed-forward), structures and process has the organisation in place to maintain the operation of its management control practices?

x. What types of use is made of information and of the various control mechanisms in place? How do controls and their uses differ at different hierarchical levels?

xi. How has the management control been altered in light of the change dynamics of its internal and external environment? Have the changes in management control practices been made in a pre-emptive or reactive manner?

xii. How robust and developed are the links between the components of management control systems and the ways in which they are used?

(Ferreira and Otley, 2009, p. 278)

Ferreira and Otley (2009) contend that these 12 questions constitute a heuristic tool to facilitate the rapid description of significant aspects of management control system development. This Performance Management and Control framework (or earlier versions of it) has been used by Stringer (2007) and Tuomela (2005) to structure case studies and write up findings. Certain criticisms of the framework should be noted, however. Malmi and Granlund (2009) point out that the framework offers little guidance on the interconnections between the questions. Collier (2005) highlights the need to understand the antecedents, background and organisational context of the design of a management control system. Their concern is that management control research may remain focused on the formal system design, rather than the system in use. Berry, Coad, Harris, Otley and Stringer (2009) argue that many of these criticisms could be overcome by using an in-depth and longitudinal field study approach, where developments in an organisation are observed over a period of time rather than a point in time, so that a range of effects of control issues are able to emerge.

Malmi and Brown (2008) argue that management control research has been fragmented in its efforts to understand the collective nature of organisation-wide management control practices. To address this situation, they developed a framework which considers a range of different types of management control practices that operate according to different principles. According to this framework there are five categories of control, which in combination constitute what they call a control package: (i) planning controls, (ii) cybernetic controls, (iii) reward and compensation controls, (iv) administrative controls, and (v) cultural controls. Malmi and Brown (2008) assumed that control is about managers ensuring that the behaviour of employees (or some other relevant party such as a collaborating organisation) is consistent with the organisation's objectives and strategy. Their model focuses on how control is exercised and, as such, it broadly maps the tools, systems and practises managers have available to direct behaviour. Malmi and Brown's (2008) analytical conception of management control as a package provides a sufficiently broad, yet parsimonious approach for studying the phenomenon empirically. Their idea of a package is to facilitate and stimulate discussion and research in this area, rather than suggesting a final solution to all various conceptual problems. They argue that the strength of their framework lies in the broad scope of the management control practices as a package, rather than the depth of its discussion of individual practices.

Broadbent and Laughlin (2009) have built on and extended the framework of Ferreira and Otley (2009) by focusing on the contextual factors that influence the workings of a management control system. Their conceptual Performance Management framework highlights the key role played by alternative models of rationality, with key distinctions being drawn between the 'relational' or 'transactional' aspects of a management control practice.

They argue that a relational management control practice is driven by the exercise of communicative rationality between stakeholders, to debate and arrive at a consensus on the objectives to achieve. This can lead to the definition of performance indicators based on substantive rationality which could, if discursively agreed, accommodate quantitative measures to typify performance indicators but more often employ qualitative indicators, with which stakeholders are more comfortable. It can also rely on transactional rationality in the choice of means to achieve such objectives, which includes performance indicators and targets. Thus, the key characteristic of a relational management control practice is that stakeholders have 'ownership' of it, which drives actions in an organisation working under a reflexive authority structure. A transactional management control practice is driven by instrumental rationality to define objectives, which take on the characteristics of being highly functional and directed to specific outcomes. In this context, 'ownership' is associated with either a particular sub-group of stakeholders or is linked to an abstract requirement that appears not to be owned by anyone. Performance indicators are defined through formal rationality, which tends to be associated closely with precise and quantitative forms of measurement. Implicit to a transactional management control practice is a reliance on legal-rational authority structures to ensure compliance. Broadbent and Laughlin (2009) argue that this typecasting of approaches facilitates a better understanding of empirical situations, as well as providing a means of evaluating management control practices by raising alternatives for comparison.

Management Control Outcomes

The development of management control practices is believed to result in a wide range of improved organisational outcomes. Yet providing a definition of a successful management control practice can be difficult. Zimmerman (1997, 2001) describes the development of management control practices as purposive and argues that it produces two distinct outcomes: (i) improved decision-making and (ii) improved control. Improved decision-making is achieved by providing information to reduce *ex-ante* uncertainty. This enables decision-makers to improve their selection of actions and thus facilitates better informed effort. Improvements in control outcomes often stem from the recognition that individuals act in their own best interest rather than that of their organisation. Management control practices therefore need to be developed by management so as to increase the probability that individuals will behave in a manner that will enable organisational goals to be achieved efficiently and effectively (Flamholtz, Das & Tsui, 1985). Management control practices are meant to serve this purpose by providing information ex-post about the actions and decisions made by subordinates. This information can then be used to change subordinate behaviour so that organisational outcomes can be more effectively achieved. Management control practices are thus deemed to achieve positive organisational outcomes if they are likely to be accepted and used by individuals, who then can approach their tasks with enhanced information.

Organisational outcomes, however, are sometimes not easily measured, and this has given rise to a host of studies that investigate different functional and dysfunctional outcomes of management control practices. Researchers have assessed the effects of management control practice on functional outcomes such as job satisfaction (Aranya, 1990), performance (Brownell & Dunk, 1991) and motivation. Chenhall (2003) categorises management control outcomes into issues related to the usefulness of management control systems, behavioural outcomes and organisational outcomes and argues that there is an implied connection between these outcomes. However, Chenhall (2003, p. 136) also contends that there are 'clear leaps in logic' made between useful management control practices and enhanced organisational performance and that the usefulness of a management control practice will depend on the appropriateness of the practice to the context of the organisation. Chenhall (2003) suggests that achieving the overall goals of the organisation and satisfying its operative goals may not necessarily be the same. In other words, attempting to align strategy with operations by translating broad organisational goals into operative goals that cascade down the organisational hierarchy can be a challenge which the literature is only now becoming aware of. Chenhall refers to the issue of complexity of goal formulation, including the difficulty of measuring particular goals, which may result in goals that are easier to measure becoming dominant. Chenhall's (2003) analysis highlights difficulties for management control that arise when multiple and competing goals, imposed on an organisation by external and internal stakeholders, may have to be satisfied.

That dysfunctional outcomes could be associated with management control practices was discussed early on by Argyris (1952), in an influential study of factory supervisors in four production organisations. The study demonstrates that budgeting induces behavioural and organisational side effects that could be regarded as dysfunctional from a management control perspective, with dysfunctional referring to outcomes that are not in the organisation's best interest. The supervisors in this study perceived budgets as sources of pressure and tension, forcing them to narrow the focus of their attention strictly to problems of their own departments. Argyris reported that subordinates felt pressured by budgets imposed on their superiors for three main reasons: the propensity of superiors to emphasise the need to meet the budget (budget emphasis); the raising of budget standards to a more challenging level once existing expectations were met; and the inflexible nature of the budget documents, which failed to disclose the real reasons for budget variances. Consequently, the supervisors expressed negative attitudes towards their superiors and towards budget procedures, which in turn caused dysfunctional side effects such as absenteeism and interpersonal conflict.

Argyris (1952) suggested that dysfunctional side effects can be viewed as individual defensive routines, meaning that individuals activate certain behavioural routines to deal with embarrassment or threat. These forms of 'individual defensiveness,' in turn, lead to the creation of organisational defensive routines, which Argyris (1952, p. 505) describes as 'any routine policies or actions that are intended to circumvent the experience of embarrassment or threat by bypassing the situations that may trigger these responses.' He suggests that the best way to overcome organisational defensive routines is to design management control practices that individuals agree are likely to be achieved, thereby signalling budget participation as a means of addressing the harmful outcomes associated with budget control. Finally, Argyris (1992) found that budget personnel acknowledged that when economic conditions were poor, budget pressure increased.

Argyris' (1952) study remains important for two primary reasons: firstly, it demonstrates the need to complement technical budgeting with knowledge of human behaviour; secondly, it suggests that dysfunctional behaviour is not just a natural human tendency, creating a need for control practices, but that it could in fact be provoked by the use of management control practices. This study was an important milestone in management control research, which now increasingly seeks to examine a broad range of outcomes associated with the operation of management control practices. Furthermore, Argyris (1952) provided a comprehensive foundation, and, indeed, motivation for future studies (Briers & Hirst, 1990). Much current research on management control in healthcare concerns itself with the question of how such controls can be designed to ensure buy-in from stakeholders. Key insights from this research are discussed in the following sections.

Recent efforts have been directed to systematise research into these unintended consequences. Franco-Santos and Otley (2018) present a review, and develop a typology to explain how and why dysfunctional outcomes occur. They report the most salient unintended consequences of management control systems are gaming, information manipulation, selective attention, illusion of control and relationships transformation. Furthermore, they argue that these consequences exist as a result of limiting factors such as ignorance, error, short-term concerns, fundamental values, self-fulfilling forecasts and changes in social relationships. The study concludes that, in the design of management controls systems, the more the 'assumed' reality about the state of goal-alignment and goal-uncertainty diverges from the 'real' state of affairs, the more the resultant system is likely to create perverse unintended consequences, leading to poor organisational outcomes. In a similar vein, Aaltola (2019) argues that this is one of the main tasks for those involved in designing management control systems to address.

Summary

This chapter introduced the domain of management control and outlined the various definitions proposed by researchers relating to it. It also discussed typologies that have been used to structure the field of study. The management control frameworks described represent a progression of thought in management control theory. Several frameworks have been suggested as research tools for examining the operation of management control practices of an organisation in a holistic manner. Finally, the evaluation of management control practice outcomes in terms of functional and dysfunctional side effects was introduced.

References

Aaltola, P. (2019). Strategic thinking and accounting: Potentials and pitfalls from a managerial perspective. *Journal of Management Control*, *30*(3), 323–351.

Abernethy, M. A., & Brownell, P. (1999). The role of budgets in organisations facing strategic change: An exploratory study. *Accounting, Organisations and Society*, *24*(3), 189–204.

Abernethy, M. A., & Chua, W. F. (1996). A field study of control system redesign: The impact of institutional processes on strategic choice. *Contemporary Accounting Research*, *13*(2), 596–606.

Anthony, R. N. (1965). *Management planning and control systems: A framework for analysis*. Boston: Harvard Business School Press.

Aranya, N. (1990). Budget instrumentality, participation and organizational effectiveness. *Journal of Management Accounting Research*, *2*(1), 67–77.

Argyris, C. (1952). *The impact of budgets on people*. Controllership Foundation, Ithaca: Cornell University.

Berry, A. J., Coad, A. F., Harris, E.P., Otley, D. T., & Stringer, C. (2009). Emerging themes in management control: A review of recent literature. *The British Accounting Review*, *41*(1), 2–20.

Bisbe, J., & Otley, D. (2004). The effects of the interactive use of management control systems on product innovation. *Accounting, Organisations and Society*, *29*(8), 709–737.

Briers, M., & Hirst, M. (1990). The role of budgetary information in performance evaluation. *Accounting, Organisations and Society*, *15*(4), 373–398.

Broadbent, J., & Laughlin, R. (2009). Performance management systems: A conceptual model. *Management Accounting Research, 20*(4), 283–295.

Brownell, P., & Dunk, A. S. (1991). Task uncertainty and its interaction with budgetary participation and budget emphasis: Some methodological issues and empirical investigation. *Accounting, Organisations and Society, 16*(8), 693–703.

Chenhall, R. H. (2003). Management control system design within its organisational context. *Accounting, Organisations and Society, 28*(2), 127–168.

Collier, P. M. (2005). Entrepreneurial control and the construction of a relevant accounting. *Management Accounting Research, 16*(3), 321–339.

Ferreira, A., & Otley, D. T. (2009). The design and use of performance management systems: an extended framework for analysis. *Management Accounting Research, 20*(4), 263–282.

Fisher, J. (1995). Contingency-based research on management control systems: Categorisation by level of complexity. *Journal of Accounting Literature, 14*, 24.

Fisher, J. G. (1998). Contingency theory, management control systems and firm outcome: Past results and future outcomes. *Behavioural Research in Accounting, 10*, 47–64.

Flamholtz, E. G., Das, T. K., & Tsui, A. (1985). Toward an integrated framework of organisational control. *Accounting, Organisations and Society, 10*(1), 35–50.

Franco-Santos, M., & Otley, D. (2018). Reviewing and theorizing the unintended consequences of performance management systems. *International Journal of Management Reviews, 20*(3), 696–730.

Henri, J. F. (2006). Management control systems and strategy: A resource-based perspective. *Accounting, Organisations and Society, 31*(6), 529–558.

Hopwood, A. G. (1974). *Accounting and human behaviour*. London: Haymarket Publishing Limited.

Langfield-Smith, K. (2008). Strategic management accounting: How far have we come in 25 years?. *Accounting, Auditing and Accountability Journal, 21*(2), 204–228.

Macintosh, N. B. (1994). *Management accounting and control systems: An organizational and behavioural approach*. New York: Wiley.

Malmi, T., & Brown, D. A. (2008). Management control systems as a package—Opportunities, challenges and research directions. *Management Accounting Research, 19*(4), 287–300.

Malmi, T., & Granlund, M. (2009). In search of management accounting theory. *European Accounting Review, 18*(3), 597–620.

Merchant, K. A. (1985). Budgeting and the propensity to create budgetary slack. *Accounting, Organisations and Society, 10*(2), 201–210.

Merchant, K. A., & Otley, D. T. (2006). A review of the literature on control and accountability. *Handbooks of Management Accounting Research, 2*, 785–802.

Merchant, K. A., & Van der Stede, W. (2011). *Management control systems: Performance measurement, evaluation and incentives*. Harlow: Prentice Hall.

Otley, D. (1978). Budgetary use and managerial performance. *Journal of Accounting Research, 16*, 122–149.

Otley, D. (1999). Performance management: A framework for management control systems research. *Management Accounting Research, 10*(4), 363–382.

Otley, D., Broadbent, J., & Berry, A. (1995). Research in management control: An overview of its development. *British Journal of Management, 6*(12), 31–44.

Otley, D. T., & Berry, A. J. (1980). Control, organisation and accounting. *Accounting, Organisations and Society, 5*(2), 231–244.

Ouchi, W. G. (1979). A conceptual framework for the design of organisational control mechanisms. *Management Science, 25*(9), 833–848.

Ouchi, W. G. (1980). Markets, bureaucracies and clans. *Administrative Science Quarterly*, March, 29–141.

Simons, R. (1987). Accounting control systems and business strategy: An empirical analysis. *Accounting, Organisations and Society, 12*(4), 357–374.

Stringer, C. (2007). Empirical performance management research: Observations from AOS and MAR. *Qualitative Research in Accounting and Management, 4*, 92–114.

Tuomela, T. S. (2005). The interplay of different levers of control: A case study of introducing a new performance measurement system. *Management Accounting Research, 16*(3), 293–320.

Widener, S. K. (2007). An empirical analysis of the levers of control framework. *Accounting, Organisations and Society, 32*(2), 757–788.

Zimmerman, J. L. (1997). *Accounting for decision-making and control*. 2nd edn. Chicago: McGraw-Hill.

Zimmerman, J. L. (2001). Conjectures regarding empirical managerial accounting research. *Journal of Accounting and Economics, 32*(1–3), 411–427.

3 Budgetary Control Challenges and Issues

Budgetary Control

Budgeting has long been viewed as an integral part of management control with proponents of budgetary control arguing that it provides a mechanism to weave together the disparate threads of an organisation into a comprehensive plan. Groot and Selto (2009) describe budgetary planning and control as the practice of developing the financial and non-financial aspects of future plans of actions by management. Budgeting is said to support organisational planning by forcing the organisation to make decisions about the quantity of resources available for the planning period and about the resource allocation to different parts of the organisation. Furthermore, budgeting is assumed to support operational planning by helping to anticipate potential problems and to prepare solutions to them.

Budgetary control begins when budgets communicate organisational objectives and planned activities to budget holders, who have responsibility and authority to implement the budget. Budgets also fulfil management control purposes by specifying objectives, targets and processes with the intent of creating better understanding of, and adherence to, organisational control, which helps budget holders in the coordination of their activities with other related organisational entities. As the budget period progresses, budgets may be used as the basis of performance evaluation. Variance analysis compares actual performance with planned performance for the purpose of understanding the magnitude and causes of the differences between planned and realised performance, related costs and revenues. Variance analysis can be used for learning, corrective actions, performance assessment and reward decisions (Marginson, 2013). In theory, then, the budget process should proceed logically through a series of sequential stages. Nonetheless, the empirical literature has recognised difficulties associated with achieving the multiple functions of budgets. The following sub-sections provide a discussion of the main issues influencing the effectiveness of the budgetary control process.

DOI: 10.4324/9781003140122-3

Accountability and Controllability

Budgetary control practices are intended to hold individuals (or sometimes groups of individuals) accountable, either for their actions or for the results they or their organisations produce. Being held accountable means that the individuals are rewarded when performance is favourable and punished when performance is unfavourable (Merchant & Otley, 2006). In an accountability-orientated budgetary control practice, it is argued that individuals whose behaviour is being controlled should be told prior to the performance period what is expected of them, and that target difficulty and ability to influence target outcome should be appropriately considered. These issues will be discussed further later in the chapter. Furthermore, after the performance period has ended, superiors should review the performance reports of what individuals were being held accountable for and reward good performance or otherwise. Consequently, rewards and punishments associated with a management control practice are seen as an important part of the management control process (Van der Stede, 2000). Rewards include things that individuals value and may come in many forms. For example, extrinsic rewards include salary increases, bonuses, promotions, praise and public recognition while intrinsic rewards stem from an individual's inner feeling, such as satisfaction and accomplishment. Punishments also come in multiple forms, including criticism, loss of autonomy, the absence of rewards that others are getting (e.g. salary increases) and even the termination of employment. The relationships between rewards, motivation and performance are known to be complex. However, there is agreement that the primary reason why organisations use reward systems is to ensure that their employees' efforts can be channelled toward activities that facilitate the achievement of organisational objectives (Flamholtz, Das & Tsui, 1985). Monetary incentives increase effort and performance by focusing individuals' efforts on a task. In addition, research suggests that linking effort to a task impacts on performance in three ways: (i) effort direction, the tasks individuals focus on; (ii) effort duration, how long individuals devote themselves to the task; and (iii) effort intensity, the amount of attention individuals devote to the task. Research has also suggested that extrinsic rewards and punishments only produce temporary compliance and that intrinsic rewards are more powerful and enduring. Nevertheless, the vast majority of organisations have implemented multiple forms of reward systems, which suggests that intrinsic rewards, by themselves, do not provide adequate motivation to everyone (Merchant & Van der Stede, 2011).

An integral element of an accountability-orientated management control practice is the application of the controllability principle (Burkert, Fischer & Schäffer, 2011). This stipulates that managers, or employees more generally, should only be evaluated based on what they can control. Therefore, if uncontrollable factors, such as unforeseen changes in the environment or decisions taken by others in the organisation, affect the results of managers these factors need to be 'nullified' in the performance evaluation of the managers concerned. This 'nullification' process can take two forms (Merchant & Van der Stede, 2011). It can occur *ex ante*, which means that performance measures exclude items that managers cannot control. Alternatively, it can occur *ex post* which involves making adjustments to remove the impact that unforeseen uncontrollable factors might have had on managers' performance. Two main arguments have been put forward to demonstrate the need for an organisation to apply the controllability principle. Firstly, it provides a reliable assessment of managerial performance. Since the profit of a division results both from its manager's efforts and from uncontrollable factors, it is not possible to consider profit as a good surrogate for effort unless the impact of uncontrollable factors is neutralised. Secondly, the controllability principle helps organisations influence individuals' behaviour because it is intrinsically linked to the idea of equity, and because fairness is considered a fundamental condition of performance appraisal effectiveness (Ittner & Larcker, 2001). When individuals feel that a management control practice is unfair they will engage in behaviour to protect themselves that might be harmful to their organisation, such as manipulating data, creating slack or developing an 'excuse culture,' using their time trying to convince supervisors that their poor performance is due to factors beyond their control (Merchant, 1989).

Despite these theoretical arguments, empirical studies indicate that the controllability principle does not always find consistent application (Drury & El-Shishini, 2005). Individuals are frequently expected to achieve financial objectives that incorporate, to varying degrees, factors they do not control, while year-end adjustments for the effects of uncontrollable factors in performance assessment reviews are only partially applied (Merchant, 1989). However, uncontrollable factors are not always easy to evaluate. For example, Giraud, Langevin and Mendoza (2008) argue it can be difficult to assess the impact of an economic recession. Furthermore, it has been argued that organisations often search for compromises between different conflicting principles, such as combining controllability with other principles like congruence (coherence with overall objectives of the company) and simplicity in managers' evaluations. Evaluating a profit centre's performance can also lead to trade-offs between the organisation's and managers' evaluation criteria. Ensuring that this is done fairly requires an ability to distinguish between those items which managers can control for and for which they should be held accountable, and those items over which they have no control and for which they should not be held accountable

(Merchant, 1989). Notwithstanding the established theoretical arguments in favour of applying the controllability principle, a vast body of empirical evidence shows that it is not always strictly implemented in practice (Drury & El-Shishini, 2005), and that it can be difficult to do so (Frow, Marginson & Ogden, 2010).

Budgetary Targets

There is a wealth of empirical evidence to support the idea that a defined, quantitative goal or target is likely to motivate higher levels of performance than when no such target is stated (Hansen & Van der Stede, 2004). There have been various laboratory-based experiments and field studies to investigate which type and level of target will produce the best performance. In an early influential study, Stedry (1960) found that actual performance was dependent on the point in the budgeting process at which the budget holder's own personal goals or aspirational level was set. Three levels of target difficulty (easy, medium and difficult) were examined. The evidence suggested that if individuals receive the imposed budget goal before setting their personal aspiration level, then their performance is highest with the difficult budget goal, because individuals adopt this goal as their own aspiration level. In contrast, if they receive the imposed budget after setting their own aspiration level, then the difficult budget goal does not result in higher performance than the medium budget goal, because individuals tend to retain the (lower) level of aspiration they choose initially. Hofstede (1967), after examining the effects of participative budgeting and budget goal difficulty, argued that budget goal difficulty has a nonlinear effect on motivation to achieve the budget. Furthermore, it was found that maximum motivation occurs when budget goal difficulty is moderate (neither very easy nor very difficult). It was also found that budget difficulty has no effect on job satisfaction, while participation has a positive effect on motivation to achieve the budget. Locke (1968) conducted a series of experiments into targets, motivation and performance, and concluded that 'results were unequivocal—the harder the goal the higher the performance.' Emmanuel, Otley and Merchant (1990) surmised that the relationship between budget difficulty and performance could be described as inverted U. It was demonstrated that performance was at its highest point (point C) when the budget level of performance results in a certain adverse budget variable. Budget levels below or above this level result in lower performance.

Empirical findings regarding the motivational impact of setting budget targets are ambiguous. Where task uncertainty is high, setting budget goals is less effective in promoting task performance than where task uncertainty is low. Shields and Shields (1998) modelled a direct relationship between three variables: (i) difficulty or tightness of standard, (ii) participation and (iii) standard-based incentives and job performance. Using the same variables, they then modelled an indirect relationship using job stress as an intermediate variable between the three variables and job performance. For the direct relationship, the tightness of the standard had a small positive relationship with performance, but for the indirect relationship, the tightness of the standard correlated with increased job stress, which has a negative effect on job performance. Overall, standard tightness had a negative effect on job performance, which suggests that tighter standards are associated with low performance.

Budgetary Participation

Budget participation is defined as a process in which an individual is involved with, and has influence on, the determination of his or her budget (Hartmann, 2000). Participation is sometimes referred to as 'bottom-up' budget setting. A non-participatory approach which tasks individuals with little influence on the target setting process is called 'top-down' budget setting. The importance of budget participation as a means of improving performance has been studied extensively in the literature. As noted above, Stedry's (1960) analysis reported that with difficult budgets, performance is improved if individuals set their own aspirations levels after, rather than before, the budget is finalised. It appears that participation in budgeting ensures an individual's mind remains open throughout the budgetary process, promoting ownership of their budgets leading to improved final results. However, the empirical evidence to support the value of participation in budgeting is mixed. Based on goal-setting theory, it is argued that the opportunity to get involved in and have influence on the budget-setting process increases an individual's feeling of control over and involvement in the budgets.

This view is consistent with Shields and Shields (1998, p. 59) who suggested that budgetary participation increased an individual's 'trust, sense of control, and ego-involvement with the organisation, which then jointly caused less resistance to change and more acceptance of and commitment to the budget decision.' It has also been argued that budgetary participation provides an opportunity for individuals to gather job-relevant information to facilitate their decision-making. Budget participation provides cognitive benefits, which enable subordinates to clarify and comprehend the means by which objectives can be fulfilled. A positive relationship between budgetary participation and job satisfaction has also been suggested. Shields and Shields (1998, p. 58) argue that 'the act of participation allows an individual to experience self-respect and feeling of equality arising from the opportunity to express his or her values.' Finally, it is argued that budgetary participation results in more realistic plans and more accurate budgets. Magner et al. (1996, p. 43) moreover suggest that budget participation 'allows individuals to introduce private information into the budgetary process, thereby enhancing the budget's quality.'

However, budgetary participation has also been associated with increased budgetary slack. Merchant (1990, p. 301) defined budgetary slack as 'the excess of the amount budgeted in an area over that which is necessary.' Lukka (1988, p. 282) states that a budget with slack is one in which the 'figure had been intentionally made easier to achieve in relation to the forecast.' Accordingly, managers will create slack in budgets through a process of understating revenues and overstating costs. The amount of slack varies over time and between companies, but it is estimated that slack might account for as much as 20–25 per cent of a division's budgeted operating expenses. Therefore, while participation has been advocated as a means of making tasks more challenging and as giving individuals a greater sense of accountability, it can also be the root of budgetary slack and poor performance.

As a result of these conflicting findings, subsequent research from the 1980s on has largely concentrated on studying factors which influence the effectiveness of participation. Hopwood (1973, p. 6) finds that task characteristics determine the appropriateness of participation and argues specifically that 'in highly programmed, environmentally and technologically constrained areas, where speed and detailed control are essential for efficiency, participative approaches' may have much less to offer. In contrast, in areas where flexibility, innovation and the capacity to deal with unanticipated problems are important, participation in decision-making was important and may offer an immediate benefit. The personality of the participants in the budgetary process also affects whether participation leads to improved performance. Merchant (1985) found that authoritarian individuals are unaffected by participative approaches, while pronounced participation was effective for individuals with a high need for independence. Studies have also explored the impact of environmental uncertainty on the efficiency of participation. Mia (1989) found that the level of participation should be commensurate with the level of job difficulty. This study shows that participation is effective when both job difficulty and environmental uncertainty are high, but that high participation is ineffective when job difficulty is low. Such findings suggest that the level of participation required to get the most from budgeting needs to be adjusted to the circumstances of the budget holder's environment (Hartmann & Maas, 2011).

Perceived Usefulness and Relevance

The importance of user perceptions of management control system design has been well recognised in the management control literature (Pierce & O'Dea, 2003). Prior studies have discussed four main attributes of management control practice design: scope, timeliness, level of aggregation and information that assists with integration (Chenhall & Morris, 1986; Bouwens & Abernethy, 2000). The scope of a management control practice refers to its dimension of focus, quantification and time horizon (Chenhall & Morris, 1986; Gordon & Narayanan, 1984). A traditional budget control practice provides information that focuses on events within an organisation and will be quantified in monetary terms, relating to monetary data. In contrast, a broad scope management control practice will provide information related to the external environment and other non-monetary factors. Broad scope information has long been recognised as being of value to individuals involved in decision-making (Larcker, 1981). However, an important finding is that the value of broad scope information can differ significantly between functional areas. Mia and Chenhall (1994) reported the perceptions of marketing individuals that showed significantly higher levels of uncertainty than those of production individuals and concluded that 'the beneficial effect on managerial performance of using broad scope MAS information is moderated by differentiation of activities in ways that isolate uncertainty within particular functions' (p. 10). Their study shows that a higher usage of broad scope information is associated with enhanced performance for marketing activities but not for production. In a related study, Pierce and O'Dea (2003) investigated the perceptions of the usefulness of management accounting information in 12 manufacturing organisations in Ireland. The findings demonstrate that individuals anticipate less need for management accounting information unless it becomes broader in scope and more flexible, timely and user-friendly. In addition, a high degree of consistency was found in the perceived deficiencies of current information, regardless of whether comments related to relatively new systems such as activity-based costing (ABC) or more traditional areas such as budgeting. In contrast, Bouwens and Abernethy's (2000) study, which examined linkages between strategic choice, interdependence and management control design, revealed that the scope dimension is not important for operational decision-making, which was contrary to their general expectation and findings of earlier research (e.g. Abernethy & Guthrie, 1994). In addition, their analysis revealed only minor differences in management control use between production and sales individuals. The issue of timeliness was the only area where a significant difference was found.

Timeliness is specified in terms of the provision of information on request and the frequency of reporting systematically collected information (Kaplan & Cooper, 1998; Pierce & O'Dea, 2003). It has been suggested that timely information enhances the facility of a management control practice to report upon the most recent events and to provide rapid feedback on decisions. Chenhall and Morris (1986) indicate that perceived environmental uncertainty influences the perceived usefulness of timely information. They contend that, in uncertain situations, individuals are likely to find that the need to respond rapidly to unpredictable events changes and, as a consequence, timely information is perceived as becoming particularly significant. Hilton (1979) modelled the value of management control information in a cost-volume-profit decision setting and found that the timelier the information, the greater the perceived value. For example, it was suggested that if information is reported monthly rather than quarterly, individuals can address concerns that arise between quarters, rather than waiting until the end of the quarter.

The third characteristic, aggregation, refers to the level and type of information provided by the management control practice in terms of its ability to supply data about cost objects that vary in size from entire divisions to individual products, components and services. Prior studies generally contend that the ability to provide sufficient detail and flexibility to allow information to be analysed for different purposes is perceived as useful (Shank & Govindarajan, 1993). Chenhall and Morris (1986) propose that management control practices that can isolate the effects of specific events on different functions are of greater use to individuals in uncertain environments. Within a healthcare context, Comerford and Abernethy's (1999) findings suggest that, unless budget control practices can identify and aggregate costs for cost-relevant objects (i.e. patients, devices, etc.) with reasonable accuracy, managers will not be able to make informed decisions on these issues. In a recent study, Pizzini (2006) examined the association between the type of budget control information provided, an individual's beliefs about the usefulness of budget data and actual financial performance. Four attributes of budget control design were analysed: the level of detail provided, the ability to disaggregate costs according to behaviour, the frequency with which information was provided and the extent to which variances were calculated. Using data from a sample of 277 hospitals, the results indicate that individuals' evaluations of the relevance and usefulness of cost data are positively correlated with the extent to which budget control practices provide greater cost detail, better classify costs according to behaviour and report cost information more frequently. However, only the ability to supply cost detail was favourably associated with measures of financial performance.

A final important aspect of management control practice design relates to the coordination of various segments within an organisation. Integration refers to the ability of a management control practice to manage the inter-relationship between segment activities. Chenhall and Morris (1986) contend that integrative information will be perceived as useful by individuals in decentralised organisations and by individuals operating in situations of high organisational interdependence.

Beyond Budgeting

In a series of articles Hope and Fraser (2003) severely criticised budgetary control practices and argued that organisations should abandon budgetary control. Their major concern was that many of the problems experienced by organisations attempting to manage their budgetary control procedures result from the fact the budget is presented as a fixed, pre-set, unchangeable target in a world of constant change and uncertainty. They concluded that budgets become outdated during the budget year, or perhaps even before the budget year begins. A review conducted by Neely, Bourne and Adams (2003) added to this theme by outlining 12 weaknesses associated with budgetary control (see Table 3.1). In an effort to overcome the problems associated with traditional budgetary control, an organisation called the Consortium for Advanced Manufacturing International (CAM-I) proposed two alternative solutions. The first of these was created by a CAM-I research group based in the US that advocated improving budgeting based upon the principles of ABC (which we discuss in Chapter 4).

The second alternative is more radical, suggesting as it does that the traditional budgetary control approach should be abandoned and replaced with

Table 3.1 Limitations of Budgetary Control Practices

- Budgets constrain responsiveness and are often a barrier to change.
- Budgets are rarely strategically focused and often contradictory.
- Budgets add little value, especially given the time required to prepare them.
- Budgets concentrate on cost reduction and not value creation.
- Budgets strengthen vertical command and control.
- Budgets do not reflect the emerging network structures that organisations are adopting.
- Budgets encourage 'gaming' and preserve behaviours.
- Budgets are developed and updated too infrequently, usually annually.
- Budgets are based on unsupported assumptions and guess-work.
- Budgets reinforce departmental barriers rather than encourage knowledge sharing.
- Budgets make people feel undervalued.

Source: Modified from Neely et al. (2003, p. 26).

a practice that evaluates managers on prevailing environmental conditions, rather than those that were assumed to exist considerably in advance of the start of the reporting period. This view assumes that the problems experienced by organisations attempting to manage their budgetary needs arise from the fact that the budget is presented as a fixed, pre-set, unchangeable target in a world of constant change and uncertainty. In addition to avoiding budgets that are outdated during the budget year, or even before the budget year begins, they advocate decentralising the organisation to its maximum potential thereby invoking a culture of trust. They assume that this will foster a greater level of transparency so that dysfunctional behaviour such as 'gaming' can be avoided (see discussion of management control outcomes in Chapter 2).

Summary

This chapter has focused on research exploring the use of, and problems associated with, budgetary control. Those arguing for the centrality of budgetary control suggest that it provides a mechanism for weaving together the disparate threads of organisational goals into a comprehensive plan and describe budgetary control as the practice of developing the financial and non-financial aspects of future plans of action. As a budget period progresses budgets can also underpin performance evaluations. For example, variance analysis compares actual performance with planned performance for the purpose of understanding the magnitude and causes of differences as well as related costs and revenue implications, and thus can support learning, corrective actions, performance assessment and reward decisions. However, where budgets are used as such attention needs to be paid to issues of controllability, accountability, target difficulty and the extent to which individuals are allowed to participate in setting the targets. Consequently, there are a number of limitations associated with the use of budgetary information for control purposes.

References

Abernethy, M. A., & Guthrie, C. H. (1994). An empirical assessment of the "fit" between strategy and management information system design. *Accounting and Finance, 34*(2), 49–66.

Bouwens, J., & Abernethy, M. A. (2000). The consequences of customization on management accounting system design. *Accounting, Organisations and Society, 25*(3), 221–241.

Burkert, M., Fischer, F. M., & Schäffer, U. (2011). Application of the controllability principle and managerial performance: The role of role perceptions. *Management Accounting Research, 22*(3), 143–159.

Chenhall, R. H., & Morris, D. (1986). The impact of structure, environment and interdependencies on the perceived usefulness of management accounting systems. *Accounting Review, 61*, 16–35.

Comerford, S. E., & Abernethy, M. A. (1999). Budgeting and the management of role conflict in hospitals. *Behavioral Research in Accounting, 11*, 93–110.

Drury, C., & El-shishini, H. (2005). *Applying the controllability principle and measuring divisional performance in UK companies.* Chartered Institute of Management Accountants: London.

Emmanuel, C., Otley, D., & Merchant, K. (1990). *Accounting for Management Control,* 2nd edn. London: Chapman and Hall.

Flamholtz, E. G., Das, T. K., & Tsui, A. (1985). Toward an integrated framework of organisational control. *Accounting, Organisations and Society, 10*(1), 35–50.

Frow, N., Marginson, D., & Ogden, S. (2010). "Continuous" budgeting: Reconciling budget flexibility with budgetary control. *Accounting, Organisations and Society, 35*(4), 444–461.

Giraud, F., Langevin, P., & Mendoza, C. (2008). Justice as a rationale for the controllability principle: A study of managers' opinions. *Management Accounting Research, 19*(1), 32–44.

Gordon, L. A., & Narayanan, V. K. (1984). Management accounting systems, perceived environmental uncertainty and organisational structure: An empirical investigation. *Accounting, Organisations and Society, 9*(1), 33–47.

Groot, T., & Selto, F. (2009). *Advanced management accounting.* Pearson Education Limited: UK.

Hansen, S. C., & Van der Stede, W. A. (2004). Multiple facets of budgeting: An exploratory analysis. *Management Accounting Research, 15*(4), 415–439.

Hartmann, F. G. (2000). The appropriateness of RAPM: Toward the further development of theory. *Accounting, Organisations and Society, 25*(4–5), 451–482.

Hartmann, F. G., & Maas, V. S. (2011). The effects of uncertainty on the roles of controllers and budgets: An exploratory study. *Accounting and Business Research, 41*(5), 439–458.

Hilton, R. W. (1979). The determinants of cost information value: An illustrative analysis. *Journal of Accounting Research*, 411–435.

Hofstede, G. H. (1967). The game of budget control: 'How to live with budgetary standards and yet be motivated by them'. *Accounting, Organisations and Society, 6*(3), 193–211.

Hope, J., & Fraser, R. (2003). New ways of setting rewards: The beyond budgeting model. *California Management Review, 45*(4), 104–119.

Hopwood, A. G. (1973). *An accounting system and managerial behaviour.* London: Saxon House.

Ittner, C. D., & Larcker, D. F. (2001). Assessing empirical research in management accounting: A value-based management perspective. *Journal of Accounting and Economics, 32*(1–3), 349–410.

Kaplan, R. S., & Cooper, R. (1998). *Cost and effect: Using integrated cost systems to drive profitability and performance.* Boston: Harvard Business School Press.

Larcker, D. F. (1981). The perceived importance of selected information characteristics for strategic capital budgeting decisions. *The Accounting Review*, *56*(3), 519–538.

Locke, E. A. (1968). Towards a theory of risk motivations and incentives. *Organisational Behaviour and Human Performance*, *3*, 157–89.

Lukka, K. (1988). Budgetary biasing in organisations: Theoretical framework and empirical evidence. *Accounting, Organisations and Society*, *13*(3), 281–301.

Magner, N., Welker, R. B., & Campbell, T. L. (1996). Testing a model of cognitive budgetary participation processes in a latent variable structural equations framework. *Accounting and Business Research*, *27*(1), 41–50.

Marginson, D. (2013). Budgetary control: What's been happening? In *The Routledge companion to cost management* (pp. 21–43). Routledge: London.

Merchant, K. A. (1985). Budgeting and the propensity to create budgetary slack. *Accounting, Organisations and Society*, *10*(2), 201–210.

Merchant, K. A. (1989). *Rewarding results: Motivating profit centre managers*. Harvard Business School Press.

Merchant, K. A. (1990). The effects of financial controls on data manipulation and management myopia. *Accounting, Organisations and Society*, *15*(4), 297–313.

Merchant, K. A., & Otley, D. T. (2006). A review of the literature on control and accountability. In *Handbooks of Management Accounting Research* (vol. 2, pp. 785–802). Elsevier: Amsterdam.

Merchant, K. A., & Van der Stede, W. (2011). *Management control systems: Performance measurement, evaluation and incentives*. Harlow: Prentice Hall.

Mia, L. (1989). The impact of participation in budgeting and job difficulty on managerial performance and work motivation: A research note. *Accounting, Organisations and Society*, *14*(4), 347–357.

Mia, L., & Chenhall, R. H. (1994). The usefulness of management accounting systems, functional differentiation and managerial effectiveness. *Accounting, Organisations and Society*, *19*(1), 1–13.

Neely, A., Bourne, M., & Adams, C. (2003). Better budgeting or beyond budgeting? *Measuring Business Excellence*, *7*(3), 22–28.

Pierce, B., & O'Dea, T. (2003). Management accounting information and the needs of managers: Perceptions of managers and accountants compared. *The British Accounting Review*, *35*(3), 257–290.

Pizzini, M. J. (2006). The relation between cost-system design, managers' evaluations of the relevance and usefulness of cost data, and financial performance: An empirical study of US hospitals. *Accounting, Organisations and Society*, *31*(2), 179–210.

Shank, J. K., & Govindarajan, V. (1993). What drives cost? A strategic cost management perspective. *Advances in Management Accounting*, *2*, 27–46.

Shields, J. F., & Shields, M. D. (1998). Antecedents of participative budgeting. *Accounting, Organisations and Society*, *23*(1), 49–76.

Stredy, A. (1960). *Budget control and cost behaviour*. New York: Prentice Hall.

Van der Stede, W. A. (2000). The relationship between two consequences of budgetary controls: Budgetary slack creation and managerial short-term orientation. *Accounting, Organisations and Society*, *25*(6), 609–622.

4 Budgetary Control in Healthcare

Healthcare Managers and Budgetary Control

There are relatively few empirical studies in the literature that assess the effectiveness of management control practices used by hospital managers, despite clear evidence that the hospital management play a pivotal role in healthcare management (Abernethy, Chua, Grafton & Mahama, 2006). Nonetheless, few empirical insights have been provided. For example, Abernethy and Brownell (1999) used data collected from 63 chief executive officers (CEOs) in public healthcare to explore the use made of budget control information in adapting to organisational change. Adopting the typology of Simons (1990), they found that organisational performance is enhanced if management control practices are used interactively. In particular, their study suggests that the interactive use of budget control information by management is effective in supporting the learning and adaptation required when strategic change is implemented. It should be noted that Abernethy and Brownell's (1999) study focused entirely on top-level managers, and the authors acknowledged that findings may be sensitive to the managerial level selected. Consequently, it would be beneficial to identify the conditions that influence the use made of management control practices at middle management level.

In a related study, Naranjo and Hartmann (2007) collected data from 218 CEOs of public healthcare in Spain, to explore how the composition of the top management team influences the use made of budgetary control practices. Their results indicate that CEOs with a predominantly clinical background focus more on non-financial information for decision-making and prefer an interactive style in using management control practices as, together, these support flexibility strategies. CEOs with a predominantly administrative background, by contrast, are more effective in establishing cost-reducing strategies due to their greater inclination to consider financial information, combined with a diagnostic use of management control

DOI: 10.4324/9781003140122-4

practices. Naranjo and Hartman (2007) suggest that healthcare performance would improve if top managers (i.e. members of the Board of Directors) actively stimulated dialogue between clinicians and management to 'demystify' management control practices and create a broader sense of ownership of them.

Finally, the study by King, Clarkson and Wallace (2010) looked at linkages between organisational characteristics, budget control and organisational performance. Based on survey data collected from 144 primary care providers, they showed that a manager's use of budget control is positively related to the size of the organisation. Furthermore, for those organisations that use budget control practices, the extent of their use is positively related to a cost leadership strategy and negatively associated with perceived environmental uncertainty. King et al. (2010) concluded that organisational performance is positively associated with the use of management control practices by administrative management in the study context.

Comparatively more significant attention has concentrated on the role of 'doctor managers' (i.e. managers with a clinical background) in the management team and the implications for management control effectiveness (Bai, Hsu & Krishnan, 2014). Empirical findings suggest that greater participation of doctors is positively associated with improved strategic decisions (Kirkpatrick, Hartley, Kuhlmann & Veronesi, 2015). In a similar vein, De Harlez and Malagueno (2016) explore how top-level managers with different personal backgrounds (i.e. clinical vs. administrative) use management control practices to successfully support hospital strategies. They suggest that the involvement of clinician managers in the use of management control practices is likely to affect dialogue between top-level managers and clinicians and is one potential solution for an effective use of control mechanisms in the support of certain hospital strategies. More specifically, De Harlez and Malagueno (2016) report that top-level managers with a clinical background, educated and socialised with different values and perspectives than top-level managers with an administrative background, would preserve freedom in professional and medical judgement and at the same time address the financial and organisational concerns of the clinicians. Finally, Lunkes, Naranjo-Gil and Lopez-Valeiras (2018) analyse hospital performance through the data from a survey sent to 364 hospital managers in Brazil. The results show that managers' clinical experience is related to higher perceived utility of management control information and historical, financial, short-term and internal information. Furthermore, through their findings they provide evidence that clinical background explains the differences in information capabilities and management control processes.

The next section discusses empirical studies examining the responses of clinicians to budget control, which remains a topic of considerable interest as clinician collaboration is likely to be central to the achievement of budget targets.

Clinicians and Budgetary Control

A considerable amount of research has been devoted to understanding the attitudes and responses of clinicians to the operation of management control practices (Cardinaels & Soderstrom, 2013). UK and American papers dominate the literature on clinician attitudes towards cost information. This research shows that clinicians have a poor understanding of the cost of the resources they use. An early study by Fowkes (1985) found that 77 per cent of clinicians in their study had no knowledge of the true costs of the drugs that they were using. O'Connell and Feely (1997) similarly found that the majority of clinicians were unable to accurately estimate the costs of the medicines they used. Ryan, Yule, Bond and Taylor (1996) found that only one-third of the clinicians in their study were able to accurately estimate the costs of drugs. They report that clinicians typically underestimate the costs of expensive drugs and overestimate those of inexpensive drugs. At a macro level, empirical studies have also examined the effects of management control practices on national healthcare expenditure. Covaleski, Dirsmith and Michelman (1993) argue that, despite various attempts at cost containment, healthcare costs in the US have continued to escalate, in part because clinician support for cost-control measures is limited.

There is evidence that the provision of accurate cost information alters clinician behaviour. For example, Cohen, Jones, Lillenberg and Neuhausse (1982) investigated whether providing clinicians with budget control information in relation to their X-ray and laboratory tests would lead to a reduction in test usage and if this effect would diminish when the feedback of budget information ceased. The study sample comprised four teams of clinicians, each working in similar inpatient units. It was reported that test usage fell during the study period in all four teams. Furthermore, in the one team that had an 'interested leader', test usage continued to decrease after the study ended. Cohen et al. (1982) concluded that the introduction of budget control information would not assure reductions in test usage. Notwithstanding, the authors argued for the necessity of educating clinicians about the potential benefits of management control information as, without this intervention, budget data will be ineffective. Eldenburg (1994) subsequently investigated the response of clinicians to budget control information in a cross-sectional analysis of healthcare. Differences in expenditure patterns were analysed in relation to the types of budget information received. The results suggest that healthcare organisations that provide clinicians with their own case costs and some comparison information have significantly lower average charges than healthcare organisations that do not. Eldenburg (1994) concluded that the provision of disaggregated information and benchmarking information is necessary to induce a 'reputation' effect that may influence behaviour and reduce overtreatment.

Researchers have also examined clinician responses to the operation of budget control practices. Jones and Dewing (1997) described a longitudinal study of a large acute healthcare organisation in the UK, which investigated the effects of management control practices in an organisation with a deeply embedded clinical culture that opposed these practices. Clinicians in the study sought to resist these practices and to continue their day-to-day activities as before. The authors admit that part of the difficulty in implementing change was the quality and relevance of management control practices. However, they also suggested that the main obstacle to successful implementation is the difficulty of effecting change in an entrenched professional culture where priorities do not reflect efficiency-related concerns. The authors proposed that the professional training of these clinicians had imposed powerful controls on their behaviour which they internalised, including an emphasis on patient welfare and a desire to adopt the best medical practice available. Control in relation to budget targets was found to be of secondary interest and was exercised only when budget targets were in danger of being exceeded. Instead, clinicians discussed control in terms of patient progression through the system, with no evidence of linkages between budget information and quantities. These findings support the earlier research by Coombs (1987) in the context of Swedish healthcare. Preston, Cooper and Combs (1992) also report the emergence of tension between clinicians and management as a result of the implementation of a management control practice. They suggest that the implementation of management control practices increases managers' awareness of medical outcomes and enables them to exercise greater control over healthcare organisations. Realising that a shift in authority can be embedded in management control practices clinicians sought to limit the legitimacy of such practices on the grounds that they inhibit or distort the exercise of professional clinical judgement.

In a study of three Finnish healthcare organisations, Kurunmäki (1999) describes how 'financial augmentation' can become an accepted practice and the language of management control has become dominant. Her study found that management control information was being used to redistribute symbolic and economic capital between clinicians and management, thereby shifting power and authority away from the former to the latter. Previously, clinicians had exercised significant control over healthcare matters through the professional freedom they enjoyed. The redistribution of power, which involved a gradual shift of control from clinicians to administrators, was regarded by clinicians as undermining their professional judgement, and an unnecessary interference with their authority. This reaction generated a strong resistance to, and covert circumvention of, management control practices by clinicians.

Broadbent, Jacobs and Laughlin (2001) further explore clinician resistance to management control practices. They found that these practices 'do not sit easily' with clinicians and they consequently use various strategies to resist them. This analysis highlights two key issues. Firstly, when clinicians perceive a regulative threat to their professional freedom, resistance is inevitable. Secondly, the actual nature of this resistance tends to manifest itself in the emergence of, as Broadbent et al. (2001) term them, 'absorbing groups.' These groups will, either internally and privately or externally and publicly, absorb and resist these changes. The choice of the absorbing group between internal and external processes is contextually determined. They conclude that this choice is likely to be related to the perceived intensity of the threat in relation to normative interpretive schemes. Overall, these studies suggest that clinicians have demonstrated an antagonistic attitude towards management control practices as these practices are perceived to be a fundamental threat to the values of the medical profession and are thus resisted. However, the picture is not entirely clear cut.

In a later study, Kurunmäki, Lapsley and Melia (2003) examined the impact of accounting in healthcare organisations. This study analysed two different healthcare contexts, in order to understand potential alternative pathways taken by these organisations and the role played by accounting practices and clinical cultures in these contexts. Kurunmäki et al. (2003) note that the incremental nature of Finnish reforms is associated with the gradual implementation of accounting processes within healthcare organisations and the progressive involvement of clinicians with them. They suggest that this context has favoured the emergence of the phenomenon of 'accountingisation.' Accountingisation describes the ability of accounting to penetrate the clinical culture and modify it. It involves the acquisition by medical professionals of accounting skills and expertise which can then be combined with their existing clinical knowledge.

In a subsequent study, also set in both the UK and Finland, Kurunmäki (2004) analysed the adoption of accounting and control systems by clinicians through a longitudinal qualitative study carried out over a ten-year period. She observed that clinicians in the Finnish setting absorbed management control information while, in the UK setting, clinicians employed management control information as a defensive shield. Kurunmäki (2004) claims that clinicians in Finland welcomed and adopted management control practices to the point that they became hybridised. She explains the differences in the accounting professions as follows:

In the UK, highly professionalised accountants have sought to, and succeeded in, retaining control over accounting practices and their jurisdiction. However, with a less formalised and powerful accounting profession in Finland, cost and management accounting have been understood as being available to any individual or occupational group.

(Kurunmäki, 2004, p. 335)

This, Kurunmäki (2004) claims, has encouraged Finnish clinicians to willingly adopt management control practices as part of their legitimate competencies leading to a hybrid profession, while the separation of spheres has remained stable in the UK. Jacobs (2005) sought to address the question of whether Kurunmäki's (2004) theory was valid in Germany, Italy and the UK. Jacobs' study focused on the education, training and socialisation of clinicians, and sought to determine if these issues needed to be altered to accord with the Finnish system where hybridisation had occurred. However, Jacobs' (2005) results contradict Kurunmäki's (2004) views on hybridisation. Jacobs challenges the assumption that there is simply a clash between the values of accounting and medicine and instead indicates that, in some settings, clinicians are willing to engage with management control practices while, in others, they delegate responsibility for these activities to a subordinate.

Kurunmäki's (2004) assertion that clinician adoption of management control practices is explained by the differential nature of the accounting profession in Finland is also not supported by Jacobs (2005), who found that, rather than a universal change in attitudes, a small group of clinicians were relatively happy to engage with the activities and responsibilities associated with management control practices. Jacobs (2005) concluded that attempts to bring about a change in clinician responses should, therefore, focus on the education of clinicians. He argued that these changes should encourage clinicians to consider how issues of cost, budget and resource management could be understood as a part of their role, as opposed to being a specialist area of interest dominated by a polarised group of clinician managers. Llewellyn's (2001) study similarly explored how the medical profession absorbs accounting information by focusing on the leadership of medical departments. Using the metaphor of a 'two-way window' to understand the aspirations and activities of clinical directors, the study reports that clinical directors simultaneously work with sets of ideas from both clinical practice and management. She concluded that clinical directors can relatively easily occupy the 'two-way space', the only issue being a lack of financial management expertise, which can be overcome by providing adequate professional training. Finally, Fiondella,

Macchioni, Maffei and Spanò (2016) explore how a transformation in the budgetary control process was implemented in a manner acceptable to those involved. The study employed a longitudinal case study of a university hospital in southern Italy, and was informed by Broadbent and Laughlin's middle range theory (MRT). The findings revealed that the change was successful due to the involvement of clinicians in the continuing process of change. In so doing, their involvement reduced their natural tendency to resist, and increased the commitment of the various groups of professionals to the novel cost-effective culture.

Contextual Factors Influencing Budgetary Control in Healthcare

Organisational Factors

Empirical research highlighting the need for management control practices to consider the organisational context has, for the most part, adopted a rational perspective. This rational perspective views management control in healthcare organisations as purposive, being so designed and implemented as to facilitate decision-making and control. Research adopting this perspective has stressed the importance of designing organisational structures and management control practices to match the organisational context.

Abernethy and Vagnoni (2004) investigated the impact of authority structures. Their study was based on survey and interview data collected from clinician managers in two large public teaching healthcare organisations in Italy. It examined the relative importance of formal authority delegated by management to clinicians, and the informal authority derived from the power and influence that clinicians maintain within the healthcare organisation. This study indicates that the formal delegation of authority to clinicians has a direct impact on the use of budget control information for decision-making. Abernethy and Lillis (2001) used data collected from CEOs and medical directors in healthcare to examine interdependencies between strategy, structural autonomy and management control design. Their analysis suggested that strategy choice had a direct influence on senior managers' decision to grant autonomy to lower level managers and that this, in turn, influenced the importance attached to measures of performance. The issue of autonomy was examined further by Silva and Ferreira (2010). They found that healthcare organisations that were financially and administratively dependent on a parent organisation were characterised by weak hierarchical controls, poor information-flow mechanisms and low levels of accountability. Their analysis indicated that a lack of direction, low motivation and, in some circumstances, poor managerial ability were key control problems in many of the organisations they studied. Their study also suggested that the strength and coherence of the links between different elements of management control practices were generally poor. Silva and Ferreira (2010) conclude that, for management controls to be effective, it is necessary to ensure that strong hierarchical controls, good information-flow mechanisms and high levels of accountability are developed to support these practices.

Studies have also explored the effects of uncertainty on the operation of management control practices in healthcare. For example, using data collected from healthcare accounting information system groups, Kim and Michelman (1990) investigated how task predictability influences user satisfaction regarding the information provided. Task predictability was defined as the number of exceptions arising in the work carried out, or the frequency of occurrence of unexpected or novel events. Kim and Michelman (1990) suggested that in healthcare, where tasks are predictable, formal administrative controls such as budget control practices are appropriate. However, where tasks are unpredictable, more impersonal forms of control and coordination were found to work best. Kim and Michelman (1990) also reported that matching the design of management control practices to the decision contexts faced was associated with improved organisational performance as measured by user satisfaction in this study. Abernethy and Stoelwinder (1995) selected a broader sample of healthcare managers, including managers of departments providing clinical services directly to patients (e.g. medical, surgical or paediatric) and clinical support services (e.g. laboratory services, medical imaging or food services). They demonstrated that budget control practices were used to a significantly lesser extent in the direct clinical departments as compared to support departments. On this basis, they argued that the judgement required for decision-making in clinical departments limits the relevance of budget control information, as these practices are based on the assumption that input-output relations can be pre-specified in financial terms.

Previously, Bourn and Ezzamel (1986) had highlighted the design difficulties associated with management control practices in UK healthcare organisations. They found particular problems associated with the identification and measurement of outcomes and the treatment of overheads. Bourn and Ezzamel (1986, p. 66) concluded that the management control practices under examination were inadequate and 'grossly incomplete', with the result that 'the quality of much of the underlying data was often dubious.' More recently, Pizzini (2006) examined, based on a sample of 277 US healthcare organisations, the association between cost-system functionality, clinicians' beliefs about the relevance and usefulness of cost data and actual financial performance. Her analysis indicated that clinician evaluations of the relevance and usefulness of cost data were positively correlated with the extent to which systems could provide greater cost detail, better classify costs according to behaviour and report cost information more frequently. However, only the ability to supply cost detail was found to be positively associated with measures of financial performance, including operating margins, cash flow and administrative costs.

Ballantine, Brighall and Modell (1998) compared and contrasted management control practices operating in UK and Swedish healthcare systems. They noted that the effectiveness of multidimensional management control practices in healthcare depends heavily on the information system infrastructure that is in place as well as the degree of integration between different organisational levels. Additionally, they found that tensions emerged in attempting to balance the provision of care with the use of financial and non-financial information. Finally, Abernethy, Horne, Lillis, Malina and Selto (2005) described how to design management control practices that actively involve clinicians and nurses. Their study adopted a multi-method approach to identify the key factors that should be considered in such design problems. They also elicited expert knowledge from relevant individuals and reflect this in the design of the management control practices they proposed. They organised key success factors into three categories: human, production processes and external factors, and proposed that each of these areas must be addressed in order for a system to meet requirements.

External Factors

Research adopting a critical/social perspective generally views the implementation of management control practices as part of a political and social regime. This regime aims to enable governments to question the prevailing modes of organising medical practices and seeks to introduce managerial discourse into the everyday practices of organising and managing healthcare delivery, very much in the sense proposed by the New Public Management reform movement. While not necessarily opposed to all such reforms, this research adopts a critical sociological approach. In particular, it often assumes that the external environment attempts to colonise clinical culture by means of management control practices, and then focuses on how clinical culture reacts to this colonisation. In so doing, this approach links closely to another theoretical school which is called critical realism. In simplified form, critical realism assumes that states and bureaucratic organisations generally seek to constrain areas of activity within their authority that question the legitimacy of their decisions and seek to counter-pose alternative value frames.

Based on a combination of quantitative and qualitative data collected in Norwegian healthcare, Pettersen (2001) found that the limited importance attached by a Norwegian County Council to the achievement of budget targets affected the way budget controls were perceived within a healthcare organisation. Since the County Council considered the budget only as a formality it did not consider the ability to stay within budget constraints as a matter of importance and did not link overspending to any penalty. As a result, clinicians equally did not view budget constraints as important, which allowed the organisation as a whole to drift away from its budget targets. Similar conclusions were drawn by Nyland and Pettersen (2004) in their investigation of the link between budget control information and decision-making processes at both strategic and operational levels in a large Norwegian healthcare organisation. They found that clinical responsibility was associated with professional ethics and norms, whereas managerial responsibility was based on individual responsibility and adherence to rules. The rhetoric used by staff suggested that management control practices were important, but that adverse performance results did not have negative effects on the evaluation of the performance of clinician managers. In fact, poor budget performance was viewed as a means of acquiring more resources. In this context, even informal feedback mechanisms such as 'coffee-room talks' could adversely affect the effectiveness of management control practices.

In a comparative study of management accounting in intensive care units in the UK and Finland, Kurunmäki et al. (2003) found commonalities and differences between the countries in terms of the problems intensive care provision experienced. Specifically, this study noted that the absence of an established management accounting profession and the willingness of healthcare professionals in Finland to assume the accountant's role were accompanied by a greater commitment to financial targets and a greater acceptance of financial responsibilities. By contrast in the UK healthcare system professionals continued to have primacy and used management control information to enhance their position. They described the resulting dynamic as '*accounting as a legitimating function*' in which accounting facts, figures and arguments were assembled to project a defensive shield around the activities of healthcare professionals (Kurunmäki et al., 2003, p. 19). In terms of responses, a study conducted by Abernethy and Chua (1996), looking at both management and clinicians, found them not only contingent on the organisation's technical environment but also on its institutional environment. When investigating attempts to introduce financial reforms in an Irish acute healthcare organisation, Robbins (2007) noted that such efforts were hampered by a lack of a robust financial information system.

Individual Factors

Considerable attention has been given to empirical studies of attempts to introduce management control practices in contexts where the pursuit of efficiency is potentially in conflict with the professional objectives of healthcare professionals. Using survey data collected from a large public teaching healthcare organisation in Australia, Abernethy and Stoelwinder (1995) investigated clinician attitudes towards budget control practices. They observed that clinicians were reluctant to accept management control practices because they were unable to identify with efficiency-based goals. Abernethy and Stoelwinder (1990), therefore, suggest that clinicians be involved in the formal management structure to allow them to gain a better understanding of the need for resource management. Building on this earlier research, Abernethy (1996) explored whether an individual's managerial orientation was more important for the effective use of formal accounting controls than the use of non-accounting forms of control. The study employed questionnaire data obtained from 63 clinician managers in four large Australian teaching healthcare organisations. Accounting controls in the study included budgeting and standard operating procedures. Non-accounting controls related to the informal interactions that occurred between organisational members during task performance. The study concluded that the implementation of socialisation strategies designed to enhance an individual's managerial orientation would improve the effectiveness of accounting controls in healthcare. However, the research also suggested that increasing an individual's managerial orientation to enhance their appreciation of accounting-based controls could reduce the effectiveness of other bureaucratic controls, such as standard operating procedures.

Comberford and Abernethy (1999) examined the conditions necessary to facilitate the effective involvement of healthcare professionals in the budgeting process. They assumed that the development of a commitment to managerial values could mitigate the potential for conflict when individuals with a high commitment to professional goals and values become involved in the budgeting process. Specifically, they propose that senior management must create the necessary level of trust if tendencies to pursue self-interest are to be contained. They argued that otherwise clinicians will be unwilling to share information or cooperate in the achievement of organisational goals and instead delay or even sabotage such initiatives. Finally, a study by Bouillon, Ferrier, Stuebs and West (2006) examined the importance of goal congruence with management control practices using a theoretical framework that draws both on agency theory and stewardship theory. Agency theory in this context relates to goal conflicts between principals, such as healthcare managers, and agents, in this case the clinicians, they rely on. Stewardship theory by contrast assumes that such conflicts are unlikely because employees, such as clinicians, are intrinsically motivated by a desire to see their organisation succeed. Their study indicated that managers, clinicians and nurses are not motivated by individual opportunism alone, and that goal congruence does not depend solely upon the selection of appropriate performance measures and incentives to remove inefficiencies and moral hazards. Rather, their study concluded that healthcare organisations realise significant performance improvement only when nurses, clinicians and management reach a consensus on strategic direction.

Summary

The literature recognises difficulties associated with achieving the multiple functions of budgets, and there is consensus that these challenges are particularly pronounced in healthcare (Kastberg & Siverbo, 2013). A consideration of the organisational context of management control follows, which assesses the merits of a purposive perspective that sees management control in healthcare organisations as being designed and implemented to facilitate decision-making and control and focuses on the need to design systems to match organisational contexts. Criticisms of this approach highlight the fact that organisational structures interact with professional hierarchies, which do not necessarily correspond with rationalisation agendas. These criticisms link to the socio-political perspective on management control which views this as part of efforts to buttress government control, while weakening traditional modes of organising medical practice, and predicts that medical staff will adopt various strategies to counter this perceived colonisation (Numerato, Salvatore & Fattore, 2012). The individual factors approach, lastly, predicts that budgetary practices pursuing greater efficiency will give rise to conflict with individual professional objectives and result in passive resistance, apathy or withdrawal by clinical staff at the personal level. We argue that a knowledge about the potential pitfalls associated with budgeting is key to developing the buy-in that is required to make these systems work.

References

Abernethy, M. A. (1996). Physicians and resource management: The role of accounting and non-accounting controls. *Financial Accountability and Management, 12*(2), 141–156.

Abernethy, M. A., & Stoelwinder, J. U. (1990). Physicians and resource management in hospitals: An empirical investigation. *Financial Accountability & Management, 6*(1), 17–31.

Abernethy, M. A., & Stoelwinder, J. U. (1995). The role of professional control in the management of complex organisations. *Accounting, Organisations and Society, 20*(1), 1–17.

Abernethy, M. A., & Chua, W. F. (1996). A field study of control system "redesign": The impact of institutional processes on strategic choice. *Contemporary Accounting Research, 13*(2), 569–606.

Abernethy, M. A., & Brownell, P. (1999). The role of budgets in organizations facing strategic change: An exploratory study. *Accounting, Organisations and Society, 24*(3), 189–204.

Abernethy, M. A., & Lillis, A. M. (2001). Interdependencies in organization design: A test in hospitals. *Journal of Management Accounting Research, 13*(1), 107–129.

Abernethy, M. A., & Vagnoni, E. (2004). Power, organization design and managerial behaviour. *Accounting, Organisations and Society, 29*(3–4), 207–225.

Abernethy, M. A., Horne, M., Lillis, A. M., Malina, M. A., & Selto, F. H. (2005). A multi-method approach to building causal performance maps from expert knowledge. *Management Accounting Research, 16*(2), 135–155.

Abernethy, M. A., Chua, W. F., Grafton, J., & Mahama, H. (2006). Accounting and control in health care: Behavioural, organisational, sociological and critical perspectives. *Handbooks of Management Accounting Research, 2*, 805–829.

Bai, G., Hsu, S. H., & Krishnan, R. (2014). Accounting performance and capacity investment decisions: Evidence from California hospitals. *Decision Sciences, 45*(2), 309–339.

Ballantine, J., Brignall, S., & Modell, S. (1998). Performance measurement and management in public health services: A comparison of UK and Swedish practice. *Management Accounting Research, 9*(1), 71–94.

Bouillon, M. L., Ferrier, G. D., Stuebs Jr, M. T., & West, T. D. (2006). The economic benefit of goal congruence and implications for management control systems. *Journal of Accounting and Public Policy, 25*(3), 265–298.

Bourn, M., & Ezzamel, M. (1986). Organisational culture in hospitals in the National Health Service. *Financial Accountability and Management, 2*(3), 203–225.

Broadbent, J., Jacobs, K., & Laughlin, R. (2001). Organisational resistance strategies to unwanted accounting and finance changes: The case of general medical practice in the UK. *Accounting, Auditing and Accountability Journal, 14*(5), 565–586.

Cardinaels, E., & Soderstrom, N. (2013). Managing in a complex world: Accounting and governance choices in hospitals. *European Accounting Review, 22*(4), 647–684.

Cohen, D. I., Jones, P., Littenberg, B., & Neuhauser, D. (1982). Does cost information availability reduce physician test usage? a randomized clinical trial with unexpected findings. *Medical Care, 20*, 286–292.

Comerford, S. E., & Abernethy, M. A. (1999). Budgeting and the management of role conflict in hospitals. *Behavioral Research in Accounting, 11*, 93–110.

Coombs, R. W. (1987). Accounting for the control of doctors: Management information systems in hospitals. *Accounting, Organisations and Society, 12*(4), 389–404.

Covaleski, M. A., Dirsmith, M. W., & Michelman, J. E. (1993). An institutional theory perspective on the DRG framework, case-mix accounting systems and health-care organizations. *Accounting, Organisations and Society, 18*(1), 65–80.

De Harlez, Y., & Malagueno, R. (2016). Examining the joint effects of strategic priorities, use of management control systems, and personal background on hospital performance. *Management Accounting Research, 30*(1), 2–17.

Eldenburg, L. (1994). The use of information in total cost management. *Accounting Review, 69*, 96–121.

Fiondella, C., Macchioni, R., Maffei, M., & Spanò, R. (2016). Successful changes in management accounting systems: A healthcare case study. *Accounting Forum, 40*(3), 186–204.

Fowkes, F. G. R. (1985). Doctors' knowledge of the costs of medical care. *Medical Education, 19*(2), 113–117.

Jacobs, K. (2005). Hybridisation or polarisation: Doctors and accounting in the UK, Germany and Italy. *Financial Accountability and Management, 21*(2), 135–162.

Jones, C. A., & Dewing, I. P. (1997). The attitudes of NHS clinicians and medical managers towards changes in accounting controls. *Financial Accountability and Management, 13*(3), 261–280.

Kastberg, G., & Siverbo, S. (2013). The design and use of management accounting systems in process oriented health care—an explorative study. *Financial Accountability and Management, 29*(3), 246–270.

Kim, K. K., & Michelman, J. E. (1990). An examination of factors for the strategic use of information systems in the healthcare industry. *MIS Quarterly, 1*, 201–215.

King, R., Clarkson, P. M., & Wallace, S. (2010). Budgeting practices and performance in small healthcare businesses. *Management Accounting Research, 21*(1), 40–55.

Kirkpatrick, I., Hartley, K., Kuhlmann, E., & Veronesi, G. (2015). Clinical management and professionalism. In Ellen Kuhlmann, Robert H. Blank, Ivy Lynn Bourgeault & Claus Wendt (Eds.), *The Palgrave International Handbook of healthcare policy and governance* (pp. 325–340). London: Palgrave Macmillan.

Kurunmäki, L. (1999). Professional vs financial capital in the field of health care—struggles for the redistribution of power and control. *Accounting, Organisations and Society, 24*(2), 95–124.

Kurunmäki, L. (2004). A hybrid profession—the acquisition of management accounting expertise by medical professionals. *Accounting, Organizations and Society, 29*(3–4), 327–347.

Kurunmaki, L., Lapsley, I., & Melia, K. (2003). Accountingization v. legitimation: A comparative study of the use of accounting information in intensive care. *Management Accounting Research, 14*(2), 112–139.

Llewellyn, S. (2001). Two-way windows': Clinicians as medical managers. *Organisation Studies, 22*(4), 593–623.

Lunkes, R. J., Naranjo-Gil, D., & Lopez-Valeiras, E. (2018). Management control systems and clinical experience of managers in public hospitals. *International Journal of Environmental Research and Public Health, 15*(4), 776.

Naranjo-Gil, D., & Hartmann, F. (2007). How CEOs use management information systems for strategy implementation in hospitals. *Health Policy, 81*(1), 29–41.

Numerato, D., Salvatore, D., & Fattore, G. (2012). The impact of management on medical professionalism: A review. *Sociology of Health and Illness, 34*(4), 626–644.

Nyland, K., & Pettersen, I. J. (2004). The control gap: The role of budgets, accounting information and (non–) decisions in hospital settings. *Financial Accountability and Management, 20*(1), 77–102.

O'Connell, T., & Feely, J. (1997). Hospital doctors' knowledge of drug costs and generic names. *Irish Medical Journal, 90*(8), 298–298.

Pettersen, I. J. (2001). Implementing management accounting reforms in the public sector: The difficult journey from intentions to effects. *European Accounting Review, 10*(3), 561–581.

Pizzini, M. J. (2006). The relation between cost-system design, managers' evaluations of the relevance and usefulness of cost data, and financial performance: An empirical study of US hospitals. *Accounting, Organisations and Society, 31*(2), 179–210.

Preston, A. D., Cooper, F., & Coombs, R. (1992). Fabricating budgets: A study of the production of management budgeting in the National Health Service. *Accounting, Organisations and Society, 17*(6), 561–593.

Robbins, G. (2007). Obstacles to implementation of new public management in an Irish hospital. *Financial Accountability and Management, 23*(1), 55–71.

Ryan, M., Yule, B., Bond, C., & Taylor, R. J. (1996). Do physicians' perceptions of drug costs influence their prescribing? *Pharmacoeconomics, 9*(4), 321–331.

Silva, P., & Ferreira, A. (2010). Performance management in primary healthcare services: Evidence from a field study. *Qualitative Research in Accounting and Management, 7*(4), 424–449.

Simons, R. (1990). The role of management control systems in creating competitive advantage: New perspectives. *Accounting, Organisations and Society, 15*(1–2), 127–143.

5 Contemporary Management Control Practices in Healthcare

Balanced Scorecard

Kaplan and Copper (1998, 1996, 1994) introduced the balanced scorecard (BSC) as a means of providing a balanced presentation of both financial and operational control measures. The BSC is premised on the idea that three different perspectives based on the customer, the internal business processes and the learning and growth perspective are of vital importance to a fourth, the financial perspective. Therefore, the BSC links customers, internal processes, employees and systems performance to long-term financial control and success. It purports that if the first three perspectives are developed in the right direction, then the fourth overarching financial perspective follows suit. The learning perspective is supposed to strengthen competence among staff members. This will support the development of internal business processes, which in turn will lead to better customer relations. Growth in customer loyalty means financial prosperity. This cause-effect relationship is essential as the three non-financial perspectives make the BSC approach a feed-forward control practice, which addresses the problem of the historical nature of traditional financial practices (Norreklit, 2000). The BSC translates an organisational mission or strategy into tangible objectives and linked performance measures, targets and initiatives.

Empirical research into the BSC has investigated the cause-effect relationship upon which the practice is premised. For example, Norreklit (2000) explored the existence of a cause-effect relationship between the four perspectives and argued that this relationship did not hold and that it was not generally the case that increased customer loyalty was the cause of long-term financial performance. Norreklit (2003, p. 615) concluded that the 'lack of a cause-effect relationship is crucial because invalid assumptions in a feed-forward control practice will cause individual organisations to anticipate performance indicators which are faulty, resulting in dysfunctional organisational behaviour and sub-optimised performance.' In a study of Finnish organisations

DOI: 10.4324/9781003140122-5

Bukh and Malmi (2005) provided evidence that organisations acknowledged the need to develop cause-effect relationships between the perspectives, yet it was evident that only a few organisations could demonstrate the relationship following implementation.

Research that examined the implementation of the BSC has raised several issues of concern, including disagreement and tension between top and middle management regarding the suitability of specific aspects of the BSC as a management control practice. Concerns have also been expressed about the use of inaccurate and subjective measures, top-down directed communication, lack of participation and inappropriate benchmarks being used for evaluation. Furthermore, research which has investigated how the BSC is used in practice has found that it was often used differently than intended. For instance, in their study Ittner, Ittner, Larcker and Randall (2003) found that future-orientated performance measures were often ignored, while financial measures were emphasised. In addition, they noted that evaluation criteria were changed, and performance measures were emphasised that did not support the desired cause-effect relationship. In the contexts studied by Ittner et al., this introduced subjectivity that resulted in favouritism and uncertainty in the reward system such that the BSC was abandoned. Epstein and Manzoni (1998) questioned the ability of organisations to agree on a strategy in such clear terms that would enable construction of a BSC. They also contended that developing and maintaining the BSC is laborious and requires high levels of senior management support to be successfully developed. However, empirical research which has investigated the BSC has found that it has been widely implemented. The success of its operation has been considered by investigating the cause-effect relationship which exists between both the organisational strategy and the BSC, and between the perspectives themselves. Significantly, Otley (2008) pointed out that the literature on the BSC had paid little attention to how the integration of target-setting, performance evaluation and reward system influences the effectiveness of the BSC, despite these issues being at the forefront of the approach.

A number of researchers have advocated the use of the BSC in healthcare contexts. Griffith (1994) nested the BSC in the broader notion of championship management and argued that it allowed the integrated management control practices to be established and performance to be tracked on several dimensions. Ganulin, Haddad and Williamson (2008) argued that the BSC was a powerful tool through which healthcare organisations could manage performance in contexts where there was a high level of operating and institutional uncertainty. Chow, Ganulin, Haddad and Williamson, (1998) contended that the BSC could help organisations guide the implementation of strategic planning, report on critical outcomes and offer a report card for consumers to make informed decisions. Oliveira (2001) stated that coupling the BSC with data-warehousing capabilities offered a new way to measure healthcare performance against its strategic objectives.

Several authors have provided normative advice for the implementation of BSCs in healthcare contexts. Chow et al. (1998) interviewed healthcare management and concluded that it was necessary to engage in a wide range of strategic management techniques. Curtwright, Stolp-Smith and Edell (2000) warned that healthcare organisations needed to develop BSCs that aligned organisational strategies with management control practices. They recommended that internal stakeholders needed to identify metrics to measure performance in each key category, so that through these metrics the organisation would be able to link its 'vision, primary values, core principles and day-to-day operations' (Curtwright et al., 2000, p. 26). Jones and Filip (2000) emphasised the need to focus on crucial processes and outcome indicators that would demonstrate how the work of all team members would impact on organisational performance.

Other researchers have been critical and have outlined problems associated with the operation of the BSC in healthcare. Zelman Blazer, Gower, Bumgarner and Cancilla (1999) investigated the concept of the BSC in relation to health centres and concluded that BSC needed to be modified to reflect the specific characteristics of these healthcare organisations. Zelman et al. (1999) identified two problems that healthcare organisations must confront when implementing the BSC. Firstly, in the model of the BSC it is assumed that an overall vision can be defined and that units within the organisation are coordinated to accomplish the vision. However, healthcare organisations are traditionally loosely coupled organisations where strategy planning and management are not as vital as in more centralised organisations. A pre-condition for the successful use of the BSC is that a common vision is created and that interdependence between different units is stressed. Secondly, the model of the BSC assumes that there are four main perspectives: the customer, the internal processes, learning and the financial perspective, reflecting the BSC's original design as a mechanism for linking long-term financial goals to performance measures and targets. However, the selection and ranking of the various perspectives have been questioned when the BSC is implemented in healthcare organisations. Pink et al. (2001) found that the perspective of the customer was given the highest priority of the four perspectives within the BSC. In other studies, a community or a visionary perspective has been considered to be the ultimate purpose of the organisation (Urrutia and Eriksen, 2005).

A limited number of studies have focused on how the BSC has been used in healthcare organisations. Aidemark's (2001) study of the use of the BSC in Swedish healthcare organisations, based on interview and archival data, found widespread support for the use of BSC. Study participants considered the BSC to be an appropriate management control practice. The BSC was seen as having replaced one-sided financial measurement with management control practice, that not only focused on balanced judgements of the organisation but also on optimising judgements. Furthermore, the BSC was seen as having reduced goal uncertainty, provided a mechanism to allow the complex work of professionals to be communicated to management and stimulated a new dialogue about vision and strategy. In a follow-up study, Aidemark and Funck (2009) examined a healthcare organisation where the BSC had been implemented for over ten years. The interview data was unanimous. During its use over ten years enthusiasm for the BSC and management control had increased. The explanation of why the eagerness to measure had not abated was summarised by noting three distinctive features: (i) decentralisation of the development of the measure; (ii) management interest, demand and support; and (iii) the flexibility of design and use of the BSC. Aidemark and Funck (2009) concluded that over time, the use of measurements led to a 'change of culture.' Measurement had become a self-evident way of approaching unanswered questions about operational processes and quality developments. Finally, Jiang, Lockee, Bass, Fraser and Norwood, (2009) argued that 'oversight' has an important impact on the operation of the BSC in healthcare. Based on a survey of managers at 490 healthcare organisations, it was demonstrated that a healthcare organisation scores better on quality in terms of process of care and mortality rates when the top managers (i.e. the board of directors) focus on performance evaluation. Additional issues related to providing higher quality of care included establishing performance dashboards with indicators for clinical quality and patient satisfaction. Furthermore, it was argued that quality performance improved when the BSC linked senior executives' performance evaluations to clinical quality and patient indicators. More critical studies such as Oliveira, Rodrigues and Craig (2020), however, highlight that balanced score card-based approaches can come with considerable costs in terms of increased bureaucracy and red-tape.

On balance, empirical research has confirmed that the theory and concepts of the BSC are relevant to healthcare organisations but that modifications to reflect the organisational realities extant in healthcare contexts are necessary. On the whole, it is not entirely clear whether or not the BSC in its original form is an appropriate management control practice for healthcare organisations (Zelman, Pink & Matthias, 2003).

Activity-Based Costing

Activity-based costing (ABC) differs from conventional costing processes in the way it treats those overhead costs which are not directly related to volume of activity. With ABC, the first stage is similar to that of the conventional cost accounting process in that it assigns direct costs of the cost object. The second stage, however, assigns overhead expenses of both the support and output activities to the activities that consume the resources. Innes and Mitchell (1995) argued that ABC identifies the relationship between activities and resources needed by assigning costs to each of these resources, thereby giving visibility to the breakdown of the total expense of the activities in their entirety. This means that ABC can be equally applied to the service industry, including the public and not-for-profit sector (Kaplan & Atkinson, 1998). This is because ABC can be adapted by linking indirect costs to the services provided through activity-based cost drivers and will thus provide more accurate costing of services.

Since its inception, researchers have advocated the benefits of ABC. For example, it has been argued that ABC produces more accurate cost information for product costing and pricing, improved cost control, more accurate performance measurement and evaluation and thus supports superior decision-making. A large number of survey studies on ABC have been conducted in different countries to determine the extent to which organisations have implemented ABC (Innes, Mitchell & Sinclair, 2000). Despite the acclaimed benefits of ABC, the results of these studies demonstrated that the diffusion of ABC has not been as wide as may have been expected. Research has attempted to explain this apparent conflict by identifying difficulties associated with implementing ABC. A major difficulty was the costly and problematic amount of work involved in implementing ABC. Shields (1995) demonstrated that senior management support, appropriate links to performance evaluation and reward systems, training, accountability and the adequacy of resources were associated with successful implementation. Anderson and Young (1999) provided empirical support for three of the factors (senior management support, performance evaluation and adequacy of training) that were outlined by Shields (1995). In addition, Anderson and Young's (1999) study suggested that user participation in ABC implementation, and their perceptions of the quality of information provided correlated positively with its successful implementation. Several researchers have argued that difficulties associated with implemented ABC systems are inherently structural. Malmi (2001, p. 461) argued that 'although sources of resistance to ABC may be numerous, they are fundamentally structural and are unlikely to be dealt with by implementation based strategies, such as participant involvement.' This aspect of research contended that ABC implementation encounters resistance simply because it threatens different stakeholder power bases within an organisation. For example, ABC implementation was found to increase the power base of factory managers at the expense of sales management and sales representatives. In a study conducted by Major (2007) ABC was implemented to explicitly meet the needs of commercial managers. However, while commercial managers were satisfied with the ABC system, the production managers and engineers who had previously been the most powerful professional group in the organisation found this emphasis on commercial managers' needs unacceptable and resisted the implementation of ABC. Similarly, Malmi (2001) found that factory managers opposed ABC implementation because the knowledge of the 'true' cost of products would have increased the bargaining power of sub-units in transfer pricing and resource allocation negotiations. While ABC is considered one of the most important innovations in management accounting of the twentieth century, surveys have shown that it has not been considered by the majority of organisations, and several factors have been identified which influence the effectiveness of ABC.

The development and diffusion of ABC principles in healthcare organisations has been widespread. Casemix funding has been the vehicle through which healthcare organisations have implemented ABC principles. Casemix funding requires patients to be classified into disease-related groups (DRGs) and for a cost weight to be assigned to each category. These cost weights assume that groups of patients within a DRG have similar patterns of resource consumption (Fetter, 1992). Cost weights represent 'prices' for the different 'product lines' produced by the healthcare organisation. Central funding authorities use the cost weights assigned to each DRG and the volume of inpatients treated in each DRG to determine healthcare funding.

Advocates of casemix funding practices have cited many favourable outcomes. For example, Duckett (1994) argued that the implementation of casemix practices had led to a more equitable distribution of financial resources. Casemix funding is also said to introduce incentives for efficiency and effectiveness. Bourn and Ezzamel's (1986) study demonstrated that healthcare organisations in which costs were higher than the prices paid for services improved performance rapidly. Furthermore, Duckett (1995) demonstrated that many of the intended incentives inherent in casemix funding practices did induce desired efficiency improvements in healthcare organisations. For example, healthcare organisations increased the number of patients treated and consequently had shorter waiting lists. The introduction of casemix funding also made a healthcare organisation's actions more visible and led to improved accountability. Increased visibility moreover provided a basis for organisational rewards and sanctions. Fetter (1992) argued that casemix funding introduced incentives for the efficient utilisation of services as well as efficiency in the production of those services and effectiveness. Individual departments could be made responsible for the efficient production and supply of the necessary intermediate services (e.g. labs tests, treatments, medication and nursing) required for the treatment of patients, whereas clinicians would be responsible for determining the mix of the healthcare's resources and services required to diagnose and treat each type of patient. Lehtonen (2007) argued that as a result of casemix funding, healthcare organisations had become better at being able to predict their healthcare costs. This study also found that some organisations had been able to compare different service providers, thereby gaining more control of the costs of specialised healthcare. In addition, clinicians had become more resource conscious and were increasingly aware of the financial implications of their activities. However, evaluation of the introduction of casemix practices has raised several general concerns. Despite the technical focus of many studies, these related to the fundamental conflict between clinicians and executive management. Data collection was identified as one such area of potential conflict. For example, it is suggested that the casemix practice is based on an algorithm which at best only explains about 50 per cent of the variation in the resources consumed by patients. Similarly, it is contended that the cost weights used were not necessarily based on sound costing principles and thus did not reflect the actual cost of treating patients in these DRGs.

Combs (1987) argued that unfavourable outcomes were associated with casemix practices, including reduced length of patient stay, growth in healthcare admissions and the de-emphasis of outcomes other than efficiency, such as quality of care. In addition to these dysfunctional consequences, concerns that casemix funding practices can lead to DRG-creeping and DRG-dumping have been raised. DRG-creeping refers to practices that aim to manipulate patients' DRG registrations in order to achieve a higher DRG compensation. DRG-dumping is where clinicians avoid treating difficult cases, because they anticipate the costs of treatment will exceed the compensation received. Empirical studies have also studied clinician perceptions of casemix funding as a decision-making tool. Lowe and Doolin (1999) found that clinicians did not believe that a more sophisticated treatment of costs was necessary and consequently were suspicious and not supportive of implementation. Similarly, Doolin (1999) explored the implementation of casemix funding in a large public healthcare organisation in New Zealand and found that clinicians had a poor opinion of the validity of the casemix information. Furthermore, they expressed little interest in using it to inform their decision-making. The disinterest of clinicians it was argued stemmed from a variety of sources. It was reported that casemix funding in the healthcare had been largely dominated by financial and costing perspectives and had produced little information of perceived clinical relevance or benefit. The low regard that many clinicians had for management control information and the occupations associated with its generation and processing also presented a major difficulty in mustering the support of clinicians. Finally, Doolin (1999) argued that there was reluctance on the part of clinicians to have their decision-making processes scrutinised with the risk that their clinical freedom might be infringed upon.

Building on the work of Doolin (1999) a longitudinal study focused on the mechanisms required to successfully implement casemix funding practices was conducted by Lehtonen (2007). This research suggested that the key to the successful implementation of casemix funding practices is the ability to persuade clinicians to become centrally involved in the management and the development of the casemix funding practice. The study suggested that integrating clinical and financial accountability and assigning responsibility for the implementation to clinicians will serve this purpose. Furthermore, freedom of choice and flexibility in adoption would, it was argued, help alleviate conflict and settle disputes. Eldenburg et al. (2010) examined a case study of ABC implementation in a healthcare organisation and reported that the observed improvements in resource consumption occurred because of extensive clinician involvement. More recently, Campanale, Cinquini and Tenucci (2014) discussed the potentialities of innovative accounting tools in supporting 'transparency' and 'resource allocation' in public hospitals, by describing the implementation of a pilot project of time-driven activity-based costing. Their findings suggest that the information produced may allow a higher coherence between resources and activities.

Benchmarking

The introduction of benchmarking in healthcare is premised on the rationale that the exchange of information about the best medical practices and associated costs will lead to greater efficiency (Jones, 2002). However, to date, little empirical research has been undertaken to support these assertions (Abernethy et al., 2006). Jones (2002) explored the attitudes of executive and clinician managers towards the adoption of benchmarking in three acute healthcare organisations. The study identified the existence of favourable attitudes towards the ethos of benchmarking. It was found that individuals believed that benchmarking sought to link cost and quality issues in a manner which was sympathetic to extant culture in the acute healthcare sector. However, evidence of inertia towards the operation of benchmarking at an operational level was found.

Northcott and Llewellyn (2005) elaborated on attempts to implement benchmarking and noted difficulties in doing so. These difficulties included gaining clinician acceptance and determining appropriate benchmarks across diverse healthcare organisations. In a different study Llewellyn and Northcott (2005) assessed the outcomes resulting from the benchmarking of healthcare costs in the UK health service. It was found that healthcare is more 'average' places as a consequence of the introduction of benchmarking. The empirical evidence showed that as doctors, patients and clinical practices were moulded into cost categories, they became more standardised, more commensurate and thus average healthcare was created. While Llewellyn and Northcott (2005) did not explicitly set out to examine the impact of benchmarking on quality they noted the potential for unfavourable trade-offs between productivity and innovation to arise, and reported other potential dysfunctional consequences associated with incentives to reduce patients' length of stay and manipulate patient-mix. Guven-Uslu (2005) investigated the implementation of benchmarking in three healthcare trusts in the UK, in which the perceptions of managers, clinicians and finance personnel towards the implementation of benchmarking were compared. It was found that the benchmarking processes which had been implemented had failed to incorporate patients and their expectations. Furthermore, Guven-Uslu (2005) contended that if benchmarking was to be beneficial in the future, local implementation programmes would need to be established.

Summary

We present the conventional view of balanced scorecard use in healthcare organisations which nests the approach within the broader notion of championship management and sees it as a means for facilitating integrated management control practices and performance tracking on several dimensions. This corresponds to our earlier observation in relation to budget control that for such measures to be successful, adaptation to local conditions and buy-in are required. More critical studies, however, highlight that balanced scorecard-based approaches can come with considerable costs in terms of increased bureaucracy and red-tape. Activity-based costing—usually implemented via casemix funding in healthcare contexts—requires patients to be classified into DRGs to which a cost weight is assigned on the assumption that groups of patients have similar patterns of resource consumption. Casemix advocates cite many favourable outcomes: a more equitable distribution of financial resources; incentives for the efficient utilisation of services as well as efficiency and effectiveness in their delivery; reduced length of stay, increases in healthcare admissions and the deprioritisation of outcomes not related to efficiency, such as quality of care. There are also suggestions that casemix funding can lead to diagnostic manipulation to achieve a higher level of compensation and dumping of patients with complex ailments seen as uneconomic to treat. However, clinicians can distrust casemix information and show little interest in using it to inform decision-making. In this vein, the successful implementation of casemix funding is reported to involve medical staff in its use and development. Finally, studies of executive and clinician managers' attitudes towards the adoption of benchmarking found they believed it linked cost and quality issues in a manner that was sympathetic to the existing culture of an acute healthcare organisation. We suggest that local adaptation and measures fostering staff buy-in are crucial success factors for the implementations of all three novel approaches to management control in healthcare.

References

Abernethy, M. A., Chua, W. F., Grafton, J., & Mahama, H. (2006). Accounting and control in health care: behavioural, organisational, sociological and critical perspectives. *Handbooks of management accounting research, 2*, 805–829.

Aidemark, L. G. (2001). The meaning of balanced scorecards in the health care organisation. *Financial Accountability and Management, 17*(1), 23–40.

Aidemark, L. G., & Funck, E. K. (2009). Measurement and health care management. *Financial Accountability and Management, 25*(2), 253–276.

Anderson, S. W., & Young, S. M. (1999). The impact of contextual and process factors on the evaluation of activity-based costing systems. *Accounting, Organisations and Society, 24*(7), 525–559.

Bourn, M., & Ezzamel M. (1986). Costing and budgeting in the NHS. *Financial Accountability and Management, 2*(1), 53–72.

Bukh, P. N., & Malmi, T. (2005). Re-examining the cause-and-effect principle of the Balanced Scorecard. In S. Jönsson & J. Mouritsen (Eds.), *Accounting in Scandinavia - The Northern Lights* (pp. 87–113). Liber; Copenhagen Business School Press.

Campanale, C., Cinquini, L., & Tenucci, A. (2014). Time-driven activity-based costing to improve transparency and decision making in healthcare: A case study. *Qualitative Research in Accounting & Management, 11*(2), 165–186.

Chow, C. W., Ganulin, D., Haddad, K., & Williamson, J. (1998). The balanced scorecard: A potent tool for energizing and focusing healthcare organization management. *Journal of Healthcare Management, 43*(3), 263.

Coombs, R. W. (1987). Accounting for the control of doctors: Management information systems in hospitals. *Accounting, Organisations and Society, 12*(4), 389–404.

Curtright, J., Stolp-Smith, S., & Edell, E. (2000). Strategic performance management: Development of a performance measurement system at the Mayo Clinic. *Journal of Healthcare Management, 45*(1), 58–68.

Doolin, B. (1999). Casemix management in a New Zealand hospital: Rationalisation and resistance. *Financial Accountability and Management, 15*(3–4), 397–417.

Duckett, S. J. (1995). Hospital payment arrangements to encourage efficiency: The case of Victoria. *Australia Health Policy, 34*(2), 113–134.

Eldenburg, L., Soderstrom, N., Willis, V., & Wu, A. (2010). Behavioural changes following the collaborative development of an accounting information system. *Accounting, Organisations and Society, 35*(2), 222–237.

Epstein, M. J., & Manzoni, J. F. (1998). Implementing corporate strategy: From tableaux de bord to balanced scorecards. *European Management Journal, 16*(2), 190–203.

Fetter, R. B. (1992). Hospital payment based on diagnosis-related groups. *Journal of the Society for Health Systems, 3*(4), 4–15.

Griffith, J. R. (1994). Reengineering health care: Management systems for survivors. *Journal of Healthcare Management, 39*(4), 451.

Guven-Uslu, P. (2005). Benchmarking in health services. *Benchmarking: An International Journal, 12*(4), 293–309.

Innes, J., & Mitchell, F. (1995). A survey of activity-based costing in the UK's largest companies. *Management Accounting Research, 6*(2), 137–153.

Innes, J., Mitchell, F., & Sinclair, D. (2000). Activity-based costing in the UK's largest companies: A comparison of 1994 and 1999 survey results. *Management Accounting Research, 11*(3), 349–362.

Ittner, C. D., Larcker, D. F., & Randall, T. (2003). Performance implications of strategic performance measurement in financial services firms. *Accounting, Organizations and Society, 28*(7–8), 715–741.

Jiang, H. J., Lockee, C., Bass, K., Fraser, F., & Norwood, E. P. (2009). Board oversight of quality: Any difference in process of care and mortality. *Journal of Health Care Management, 54*(1), 15–30.

Jones, C. S. (2002). The attitudes of British National Health Service managers and clinicians towards the introduction of benchmarking. *Financial Accountability & Management, 18*(2), 163–188.

Jones, M. L., & Filip, S. J. (2000). Implementation and outcomes of balanced scorecard model in women's services in an academic health care institution. *Quality Management in Health Care, 8*(4), 40–51.

Kaplan, R. S. (1994). Management accounting (1984–1994): Development of new practice and theory. *Management Accounting Research, 5*(3–4), 247–260.

Kaplan, R. S., & Cooper (1996). *Translating strategy into action: The balanced scorecard*. Boston: Harvard Business School Press.

Kaplan, R. S., & Atkinson, A. (1998). *Advance management accounting* (Third edn). Prentice Hall International: Boston, Massachusetts.

Kaplan, R. S., & Cooper, R. (1998). *Cost and effect: Using integrated cost systems to drive profitability and performance*. Boston: Harvard Business School Press.

Lehtonen, T. (2007). DRG-based prospective pricing and case-mix accounting—exploring the mechanisms of successful implementation. *Management Accounting Research, 18*(3), 367–395.

Llewellyn, S., & Northcott, D. (2005). The average hospital. *Accounting, Organisations and Society, 30*(6), 555–583.

Lowe, A., & Doolin, B. (1999). Casemix accounting systems: New spaces for action. *Management Accounting Research, 10*(3), 181–201.

Major, M. (2007). Activity-based costing and management: A critical review. *Issue in Management Accounting* (3rd edn, pp. 155–174). Harlow: Prentice Hall.

Malmi, T. (2001). Balanced scorecards in Finnish companies: A research note. *Management Accounting Research, 12*(2), 207–220.

Norreklit, H. (2000). The balance the balanced scorecard: A critical analysis of some of its assumptions. *Management Accounting Research, 11*(1), 65–88.

Norreklit, H. (2003). The balanced scorecard: What is the score? A rhetorical analysis of the balanced scorecard. *Accounting, Organisation and Society, 28*(6), 591–619.

Northcott, D., & Llewellyn, S. (2005). Benchmarking in UK health: A gap between policy and practice? *Benchmarking: An International Journal, 12*(5), 419–435.

Oliveira, H. C., Rodrigues, L. L., & Craig, R. (2020). Bureaucracy and the balanced scorecard in health care settings. *International Journal of Health Care Quality Assurance*.

Oliveira, J. (2001).The Balanced Scorecard: An integrative approach to performance evaluation. *Healthcare Financial Management, 55*(May), 42–46.

Otley, D. (2008). Did Kaplan and Johnson get it right? *Accounting, Auditing and Accountability Journal, 21*(2), 229–239.

Pink, G., McKillop, I., Schraa, E., Preyra, C., Montgomery, C., & Baker, G. R. (2001). Creating a balanced scorecard for a hospital system. *Journal of Health Care Finance, 27*(Spring), 1–20.

Shields, M. D. (1995). An empirical analysis of firms' implementation experiences with activity-based costing. *Journal of Management Accounting Research, 7*(1), 148–165.

Urrutia, I., & Eriksen, S. D. (2005). Application of the balanced scorecard in Spanish private health-care management. *Measuring Business Excellence*.

Zelman, W. N., Blazer, D., Gower, J. M., Bumgarner, P. O., & Cancilla, L. M. (1999). Issues for academic health centres to consider before implementing a balanced-scorecard effort. *Academic medicine: Journal of the Association of American Medical Colleges, 74*(12), 1269–1277.

Zelman, W. N., Pink, G. H., & Matthias, C. B. (2003). Use of the balanced scorecard in health care. *Journal of Health Care Finance, 29*(4), 1–16.

6   Virtual Healthcare Delivery and Management Control

Virtual Healthcare Delivery and Management Control

The outbreak of the COVID-19 pandemic has meant that the implementation of virtual healthcare delivery has become a dominant issue within the healthcare management literature. This has not meant that other important topics have disappeared, but it has provoked a re-evaluation in light of their potentially important contribution to the widely predicted expansion of virtual healthcare provision. This situation is not surprising, since virtual healthcare provision promises to provide at least an improved response to a number of problems the current pandemic has created. Virtual healthcare systems may facilitate more interactions with healthcare consumers, and contribute to the swift training and subsequent deployment of additional staff. Some researchers have advocated the replacement of personal service provision with virtual systems. Indeed, services such as repeat prescriptions for chronically ill patients, for whom access to conventional facilities (pharmacies or GP offices) now has become more difficult or risky, are now being provided via smart phones and computers. Most importantly, there is the expectation that telehealth or virtual healthcare will help flatten the COVID-19 infection curve (Leite, Gruber & Hodgkinson, 2020), or at least help manage or mitigate the dangerous bottlenecks that can arise when essential healthcare personnel are infected by those they treat. Perhaps not surprisingly, a number of researchers are predicting the rise of new generations of telepractitioners (Campbell & Goldstein, 2021). Others foresee the rapid deployment of virtual approaches aimed at improving access to services, while providing differentiated and sophisticated, networked service offerings. These optimistic views for the future of tele- and virtual health are based on an observed increase in regulatory and legislative support, greater acceptance by consumers, technical advancements within telehealth platforms and the promise that they will contribute to the resilience of healthcare systems (Gupta et al., 2020). For the purpose of this chapter,

DOI: 10.4324/9781003140122-6

which focuses on these developments and telemedicine more generally, we utilise the following conventional definition of tele- or virtual health:

> Telehealth is understood to comprise electronic and telecommunications technologies and services in the provision of care and health services at a distance, within which telemedicine as a practice of medicine using technology to deliver care at a distance might also be adopted.
>
> (Leite, Gruber & Hodgkinson, 2020, p. 222)

This broad definition of telehealth is useful because of its emphasis on distance, which obviously encapsulates the enhanced potential of these technologies in times of an infectious pandemic. It is also useful in that it leaves open the specific use for which technology is employed and as such includes technologies for tracking, testing and treating (3Ts) patients, as a set of strategic actions that are helping healthcare systems and governments manage the spread of the virus (Mayor, 2020; Smith et al., 2020; Leite, Gruber & Hodgkinson, 2020, p. 222). Due to the novelty of this literature this chapter will both include references to the academic literature in the field as well as point to contributions from the rapidly developing grey literature in the area.

Although notions and technologies associated with tele- or virtual healthcare are now broadly understood this was not always the case. In the past misunderstandings of these approaches arose, as early writers in the area frequently intermingled discussions of telehealth—which were mostly about overcoming distance through the use of technology—with notions of personalised medicine or individualised or person-centred medicine (PCM), which were closely associated with the expectation that future developments in pharmaceutical technology would lead to the creation of individualised medications (Dorman et al., 2004; Shastry 2006). The personalised medicine literature was also about technology-enabled medical provision but did not attach the same centrality to physical distance. For the purpose of this chapter, we assume that terms such as virtual health, e-health, telehealth, telemedicine and connected health refer to basically similar or identical developments, whereas individualised medicine, personalised medicine and PCM are distinct phenomena, relating to the tailoring of medicine to individual needs which may or may not include the use of technology for overcoming or coping with physical distance or facilitating physical access.

In parallel to drawing out clearer distinctions between telehealth and other technology-driven healthcare innovations, the contemporary telehealth literature tends to encourage healthcare policy makers to move away from the techno-centric perspectives of 'medical informatics' or 'healthcare informatics' to embrace connected health systems that might be characterised as consumer or patient orientated. Such connected systems tend to emphasise the needs of consumers, and continuity of care alongside the integration of social and healthcare services. They also prioritise access for various patient groups, and the creation of disease-orientated networks (see Rossimori, Mercurio & Verbicaro, 2012, p. 4 and p. 7). In so doing they respond to changes in demographic and cultural factors that will facilitate the dissemination of innovations associated with telehealth, telehome care or home telehealth and connected health. Pre-COVID-19, it was assumed that these processes would be driven by the growing healthcare needs of an aging population (Koch, 2006, p. 566), increased lifestyles associated chronic diseases, and greater demand for accessible care within and outside hospitals. Even before the COVID-19 pandemic, the limited financial resources of some healthcare systems and difficulties in staff recruitment and retention in the healthcare services—in home and elderly care in particular—were seen as favouring the adoption of the methods involving communication technology (Koch, 2006, p. 566). The advent of COVID-19 has given further impetus to the application of virtual approaches to healthcare delivery. Thus, there has been a recognition early on in the pandemic that care in hospitals created potentially dangerous vectors of infection transmission that could be mitigated via greater employment of home care, which telehealth technology could facilitate (Senni, 2020; Leva et al., 2020).

Telehealth and Virtual Health: Origins, Evolution and Key Approaches

The word 'telehealth' was originally used to describe the use of modern communication technologies such as e-mail, interactive e-mail and video-conferencing in the delivery of health services (McCarty & Clancy, 2002, p. 153). Definitions of telehealth, connected or virtual health vary considerably, and show a good deal of overlap, which has given rise to the suggestion that differences may largely be due to regional usage. Usage suggests a predominance of the term 'telehealth' within the American literature, while connected or virtual health appears to have wider usage in the continental European literature.

A detailed review by Koch (2006, p. 565) found the bulk of publications on telehealth and connected health (44 per cent) to come from the United States, followed by the United Kingdom and Japan. In terms of themes, Koch (2006, p. 565) found that research on telehealth focused on two areas—vital sign parameter (VSP) measurement and audio/video consultations (virtual visits)—with clinical application domains focusing on chronic diseases, elderly patients and paediatrics. Other areas of telehealth research appear to be less developed. This includes matters of improved information access and communication underpinning and providing decision support to staff, patients and relatives (Koch, 2006). Telehealth-related research on diagnosis and delivery has strongly impacted on definitions of this growing branch of healthcare (Steventon et al., 2012, p. 2). Accordingly, telehealth has been defined as being characterised by the 'remote exchange of data between a patient and healthcare professionals as part of the patient's diagnosis and health care management' (Sventon et al., 2012a, p. 2, citing McLean, Protti & Sheikh, 2011; see also Sood et al., 2007).

A number of what are felt to be important applications of virtual health such as 'the monitoring of blood pressure and blood glucose' and other measures which 'may help patients to better understand their health conditions by providing tools for self-monitoring, are expected to encourage better self-management of health problems, and alert professional support if devices signal a problem' (Sventon et al., 2012, p. 2). This underpins expectations that virtual health will deliver 'appropriate care for each patient' and support the efficient use of healthcare resources by 'reducing the need for expensive hospital care' (Sventon et al., 2012, p. 2). Taking a similar view (that is, telehealth should encourage and facilitate self-care in conjunction with interventions by healthcare practitioners) some researchers have described connected health as the endpoint of a cultural evolution which they claim began in the 1970s when 'medical informatics' first attracted professional attention. Medical informatics was initially seen as sub-discipline of computer science. It broadened out into a new field that became known as 'healthcare informatics' in the 1980s with the realisation that medical practice needed to be extended to organisational contexts in which virtual healthcare approaches were embedded (Rossimori, Mercurio & Verbicaro, 2012, p. 6).

Yet more terminology was introduced by the European Commission, which made 'Information and Communication Technology (ICT) for health' a funding priority in the 1990s. This was meant to reflect the fact that the internet enabled two-way exchanges of healthcare-relevant information between patients and healthcare providers (Rossimori et al., 2012, p. 6). The clumsy 'ICT for health' was replaced in 2000 in European-government action plans by the new streamlined term 'e-health' that bore some similarity to the US coined notion of 'telehealth', which now had also found occasional use in European academic writing (Rossimori et al., 2012, p. 7). E-health in turn has been gradually replaced by 'connected' or 'virtual' health, which many researchers thought preferable because of the implied reference to the health needs of patients and healthcare consumers more generally (Rossimori et al., 2012, p. 7). The different designations that the various systems go by should not obscure how much they share in common. Differences relating to notions of 'connected' or 'virtual' health and 'telehealth' are probably relatively minor, and reflect the greater focus in the US literature on technological or telehealth platforms as compared to the focus of the European health literature on the connection of patients to each other and to healthcare providers. Following this trajectory, a recent definition of connected health describes it as the

> new and emerging application of internet, mobile and wireless technologies to: (i) 'connect' the patient to expert advice and information knowledge databases, ii) 'connect' patients to each other in self-help groups, iii) 'connect' the patient to monitoring devices for self-diagnosis, iv) 'connect' the patient's physiological measurements and data.
> (Nyberg, Xiong & Loustarinen, 2011, p. 220)

Models of Virtual Healthcare Delivery

Following the COVID-19 outbreak, the application of telehealth/connected health to homecare, that is, their deployment in patients' homes, has become particularly important. This is sometimes described as tele-homecare, home telehealth or home-based e-health (Koch, 2006, p. 566). Even before COVID-19, home telehealth had become a particularly relevant area for telehealth advocates, as can be seen from research into examples of large-scale, well-documented, successful and workable applications in this area (Melo & Beck, 2014). Central to home telehealth—now widely employed in the US—is the telehomecare visit; 'a two-way interactive audio-visual communication between a healthcare provider and a patient in his/her place' that may entail a 'physical assessment of the patient's heart, lung and bowel sounds and obtaining vital signs, such as blood pressure and pulse' (Koch, 2006, p. 566). According to the *US Department of Veterans Affairs* (the largest and most advanced telehealth provider), in terms of both quantity of services provided and analytical understanding of their efficacy (Tuerk et al., 2010), '[t]elehomecare … involves a comprehensive patient/family health education program with a strong component of self-management of chronic illnesses' as well as 'less complex, non-interactive technology', giving 'patients the opportunity to report, via internet, modem or telephone, disease specific symptoms' (Koch, 2006, p. 2). In many ways tele-homecare provision by the US Department of Veterans Affairs is today considered the pinnacle of what telehealth can accomplish, as well as being an undisputed success story in terms of efficiency and the quality of care afforded to patients. Needless to say, these positive views, which initially rested primarily on cost and service quality considerations—and especially reductions in hospital admissions—have been re-enforced by that system's advantages in the context of the current pandemic. Remote distance aspects of homecare provision reduce risks to patients and healthcare professionals alike, while allowing more patients to be offered services (Car, Koh, Foong & Wang, 2020). The grey literature documents how the utilisation of telehealth during the current pandemic facilitated communication with healthcare users (Syed, 2021) in addition to allowing for the inclusion of COVID-19-related services in existing packages (Vincent, 2021).

Early developments in telehealth were motivated by the desire to provide health services to inhabitants of rural and remote areas of Canada and the US (McCarthy & Clancy 2002, p. 153, citing Bashshur, 1997). Early applications, starting in 1948, involved the transmission of radiological imagesby telephone, healthcare providers branched out to use available technology such as video in interactive therapy. In the 1990s, the decreasing costs and increased efficiency of technologies such as the World Wide Web brought renewed interest in telehealth applications to government agencies (McCarthy & Clancy, 2002, p. 153; citing Whitten & Collins, 1997). This then led to studies which examined the experiences of patients and the healthcare workforce in relation to telehealth/connected health, and documented largely positive experiences in terms of healthcare quality and cost. A large-scale project that attracted global attention was the US Veterans Health Administration national home telehealth programme—the Care Coordination/Home Telehealth (CCHT).

The CCHT was preceded by smaller scale pilots of home telehealth projects to provide care to patients with chronic diseases. When it was eventually rolled out, CCHT attracted broad interest because of its successful implementation and outcomes. Evaluations suggested early on that CCHT represented 'a practical and cost-effective means of caring for populations of patients with chronic disease that was acceptable to both patients and clinicians' (Darkins et al., 2008, p. 1118). Interest in CCHT extended to the UK, not least because the NHS employs organisational and payment structures which are in some ways comparable to the Veterans Administration's health services (Cruickshank, 2012), albeit that the VA operates on a much smaller scale of about 300,000 patients. The VA's CCHT had been introduced between 2003 and 2007. By 2007 there were 31,560 veteran patients using the system. Of these 95 per cent were males over 65 years old with chronic conditions, using the system to coordinate their care needs and thereby avoiding unnecessary admissions to long-term institutional care (Darkins et al., 2008, p. 1118). By 2010, enrolment figures for CCHT had grown to ca. 70,000 patients (Broderick, 2013). Evaluations noted that CCHT's success was due primarily to two main guiding principles: (i) the selection, by a care coordinator, of 'appropriate home telehealth technology', and (ii) acquisition of required training by patients and caregivers (Darkins et al., 2008, p. 1120). Additional elements included 'reviews of telehealth monitoring data, and ... [ongoing] active care or case management (including communication with the patient's physician)' (Darkins et al., 2008, p. 1120). The choice of monitoring technology and user interface, meanwhile, was based on a series of criteria, including 'a patient's health needs, the complexity of disease/condition, and [their] ability to use technology' (Darkins et al., 2008, p. 1120). Although economic evaluations of the CCHT have tended to focus on cost-relevant parameters, such as the ability of a care coordinator to manage 'a panel of between 100 and 150 general medical patients or 90 patients with mental health-related conditions' (Darkins et al., 2008, p. 1120) and its low cost of '$1,600 per patient per annum' (Darkins et al., 2008, p. 1118), there is evidence that the programme does indeed entail strong aspects of patient centredness, with high levels of patient satisfaction (Young, Foster, Silander & Wakefield, 2011) and reduced mortality (Darkins, Kendall, Edmonson, Young & Stressel, 2015). These advantages of CCHT appear to be rated particularly highly among patients living in rural and remote areas (Luptak et al., 2010).

In terms of hard medical data, a cohort of 17,025 CCHT patients showed 'a 25 percent reduction in numbers of bed days of care' and a '19 percent reduction in numbers of hospital admissions' (Darkins et al., 2008, p. 1118). Influenced by CCHT, the UK has funded a randomised trial study of a demonstrator cluster (Steventon et al., 2012). The study involved 3,230 people with diabetes, chronic obstructive pulmonary disease and heart failure who were recruited from practices between May 2008 and November 2009 (Steventon et al., 2012). The study initially appeared to confirm the non-randomised observations made in connection with CCHT, observing significantly lower rates of hospital admissions, and emergency admissions in particular, for those who were provided with telehealth support. Additionally, there was evidence of lower mortality among the telehealth-supported group. These findings were released as 'one of five analyses, and reports on how telehealth affected the use of secondary healthcare and mortality' (Steventon et al., 2012, p. 2). Other analyses of the demonstrator cluster were meant to 'assess how telehealth affected quality of life and cost effectiveness, and explore the patient, professional, and organisation factors related to implementation' (Steventon et al., 2012, p. 2). Unfortunately, a more detailed examination of the British data identified a number of design flaws in the study and its interpretation. Thus, although the Whole Systems Demonstrator (WSD) trial found that telehealth was associated with lower rates of emergency hospital admissions than usual amongst patients with long-term health conditions, admission rates increased amongst the control group shortly after recruitment, leading to concerns about whether the estimated treatment effect reflected telehealth or was an artefact of the trial (Steventon et al., 2012). When the results of the British study were eventually released, it was with the caveat that 'when delivered properly telehealth/telecare could potentially deliver positive results' (The King's Fund, 2011). It is likely that the somewhat inconclusive results of the NHS study put a dampener on the UK NHS's appetite for telehealth. Another explanation, however, is that the UK government under David Cameron had become aware of the considerable initial investment cost a nationwide telehealth programme targeting chronic disease sufferers would entail. The authors of this book would expect the issue to be revisited within the next couple of years, if only on account of the ability of telehealth to increase healthcare system resilience in times of crisis, such as the current COVID-19 pandemic.

Telehealth, Virtual Health and Management Control

While there is now ample research on the steps involved in the implementation of telehealth programmes as well as a good understanding of measures involved in developing and implementing virtual health initiatives including the associated capital investments, personnel and training requirements (see, e.g. Rashvand & Hsiao, 2018), far less is known about management control and performance aspects of virtual health initiatives. This in part not only reflects the relatively recent age of these approaches but also the fact that their development has been driven by large organisations such as the US Veterans Administration (VA) that could draw on significant resources when it came to initial capital investments. This situation has changed only recently on account of two main factors. Firstly, organisations such as the VA have now conducted their initial investment and are more eager to observe running costs and evaluate management issues more generally. Secondly, there has been an interest among private and semi-private sector organisations in providing virtual health services, which has led to greater cost-awareness and also a general increase in interest in the managerial performance aspects associated with these approaches.

The first major academic study of performance aspects of telemedicine was authored by two members of the *US Marine Corps* working at *Walter Reed Army Medical Centre (WRAMC)* and appeared in the journal *Military Medicine* (Eliasson & Poropatich, 1998). This pioneering work places performance aspects associated with telemedicine in the broad context of quality management in medicine, which follows the approach taken by the US Institute of Medicine and a number of textbooks in the area (Field, 1996). This approach emphasises the disaggregation of activities into discrete components. For specific components, performance improvement initiatives can then be applied. According to this rationale, performance initiatives then involve the following steps which they summarise as the FOCUS method (Eliasson & Poropatich, 1998, p. 533):

a) Finding a process that needs to be addressed or fixed—that is perceived as suboptimal by comparison to other existing telemedicine activities—this is denoted by the acronym 'F.'
b) Organising a team composed of important owners of the process to be addressed which is denoted by the acronym 'O.'
c) Clarifying current knowledge about the chosen improvement project, and if current knowledge is insufficient, gathering more information before the next step which is denoted by the acronym 'C.'
d) Understanding the causes of variation by using a number of useful tools such as fishbone diagrams, organisational charts, and Pareto diagrams; this is denoted by the acronym 'U.'
e) Finding, piloting and implementing a solution which is denoted by the acronym 'S.'

Among telemedicine practitioners it is well understood that effective performance improvement initiatives, whether they use the aforementioned FOCUS approach or not, will usually require the commitment of additional resources to existing telemedicine initiatives. This includes the management of the performance initiative itself which can put demands on the entire organisation and all members who are empowered to contribute. This in a sense makes the careful selection of an area for performance improvement one of the most important steps. Telemedicine practitioners would therefore argue that areas for improvement should be chosen with do-ability in mind and also with a view toward maximising overall positive effects on the existent service offering. Assuming that some of the core issues of telemedicine provision, including licensing and credentialing as well as data security and privacy, have been successfully and satisfactorily addressed, peer review can then become the backbone of high-level internal management control. Eliasson and Poropatich (1998, p. 532) argue that 'Peer review, including an effective feedback mechanism to the reviewed provider, is accepted in medical practice.' While Eliasson and Poropatich (1998, p. 532) suggest that 'Practitioners in a health care system tend to recognize the value of participating in peer review as long as they participate in designing the objective review criteria to be used', they warn that this can be a particular challenge in telemedicine contexts. This is the case because it requires electronic medical records to be stored and shared and evaluated. This by itself poses significant requirements in terms of data fidelity and security. Eliasson and Poropatich (1998, p. 533), however, further note that to be effective 'Feedback from peer review must be provided in an unambiguous and timely fashion. Results of peer review need to be recorded by provider name and kept in a file for each practitioner. They also suggest (1998, p. 533) 'This information must be readily available to the chief of the clinical service so that it may be reviewed at times of career counselling, consideration for promotion, and credentialing.' They conclude that properly performed peer review is more valuable than the licensing process and that well-documented feedback mechanisms can underpin credentialing as well as support quality and performance improvement initiatives. As a means of coping with the workload this entails, Eliasson and Poropatich (1998, p. 533) suggest sampling and also the editing of records to a manageable length (see also Gomez, Poropatich, Karinch & Zajtchuk, 1996).

While most of the literature on telemedicine has focused on implementation and management aspects of virtual health activities, some recent contributions have sought to address commercial aspects (see e.g. Mark & Augenstein, 2019). While diverse in nature and content this literature typically highlights high upfront costs as well as initial investment costs, and downstream savings and efficiency gains by comparison to traditional non-virtual approaches. The literature also tends to emphasise skill requirements for staff and personnel costs as key running expenditure. In terms of practical recommendations, considerable implementation potential for telehealth initiatives is seen for academic medical centres that can provide some types of specialist services remotely, some types of services provided by community hospitals and primary care clinics. In terms of activities, it is thought that patient satisfaction and health outcomes can be improved by offering direct-to-consumer telehealth services for low-acuity conditions, while patients can be better connected to behavioural health and speciality care through virtual visits. Lastly, there is an expectation that costs can be reduced via remote monitoring of several groups of patients with chronic conditions (Briggs, 2018). In many respects research in these areas is still evolving and the understanding of the managerial challenges telemedicine poses is likely to develop alongside the implementation of new initiatives and applications. In any case, telemedicine is likely to remain one of the most promising and fast-developing areas of healthcare for many years to come.

References

Bashshur, R. L. (1997). Telemedicine and the health care system. In R. Bashshur, J. H. Sanders, & G. W. Shannon (Eds.), *Telemedicine: Theory and practice* (pp. 5–33). Springfield: Charles C. Thomas.

Briggs, K. (2018). Harnessing the power of connected care and telehealth. *Health Management, 18*(1). Available from: https://healthmanagement.org/c/healthmanagement/issuearticle/harnessing-the-power-of-connected-care-and-telehealth-1 (accessed 20 January 2020).

Broderick, A. (2013). The Veterans Health Administration: Taking home telehealth services to scale nationally. In *Case Studies in Telehealth Adoption* (p. 4). Commonwealth Fund publishing, 1657.

Campbell, D. R., & Goldstein, H. (2021). Genesis of a new generation of telepractitioners: The COVID-19 pandemic and paediatric speech-language pathology services. *American Journal of Speech-Language Pathology, 30*(5), 2143–2154.

Car, J., Koh, G. C. H., Foong, P. S., & Wang, C. J. (2020). Video consultations in primary and specialist care during the covid-19 pandemic and beyond. *British Medical Journal, 371.*

Cruickshank, J. (2012). *Telehealth: What can the NHS learn from the US Veterans Health Administration.* London: Health.org.

Darkins, A., Kendall, S., Edmonson, E., Young, M., & Stressel, P. (2015). Reduced cost and mortality using home telehealth to promote self-management of complex chronic conditions: A retrospective matched cohort study of 4,999 veteran patients. *Telemedicine and e-Health, 21*(1), 70–76.

Darkins, A. D., Ryan, P., Kobb, R., Foster, L., Edmonson, E., Wakefield, B., & Lancaster, A. E. (2008). Care Coordination/Home Telehealth: The systematic implementation of health informatics, home telehealth, and disease management to support the care of veteran patients with chronic conditions. *Telemedicine and e-Health, 14*(10), 1118–1126.

Dormann, H., Neubert, A., Criegee-Rieck, M., Egger, T., Radespiel-Troger, M., Evans, W. E., & Relling, M. V. (2004). Moving towards individualised medicine with pharmacogenomics. *Nature, 429,* 464–468.

Eliasson, A. H., & Poropatich, R. K. (1998). Performance improvement in telemedicine: The essential elements. *Military Medicine, 163*(8), 530–535.

Field, M. J. (1996). *Telemedicine: A guide to assessing telecommunications in health care.* Washington, DC: National Academy Press.

Gomez, E., Poropatich, R., Karinch, M. A., & Zajtchuk, J. (1996). Tertiary telemedicine support during global military humanitarian missions. Telemedicine Journal, *2,* 201–10.

Gupta, A., Baird, M., Vyas, S., Reich, J., Zawada, S., Nagpal, S., & Mechanic, O. J. (2020). Predictions for Telehealth in 2020: Will this be the takeoff year? *Telehealth and Medicine Today.* 2020 Jan 31; 5(1).

Koch, S. (2006). Home telehealth: Current state and future trends. *International Journal of Medical Informatics, 75,* 565–576.

Leite, H., Hodgkinson, I. R., & Gruber, T. (2020). New development:'Healing at a distance'—telemedicine and COVID-19. *Public Money & Management, 40*(6), 483–485.

Leva, E., Morandi, A., Sartori, A., Macchini, F., Berrettini, A., & Manzoni, G. (2020). Correspondence from Northern Italy about our experience with COVID-19. *Journal of Pediatric Surgery, 55*(5), 985.

Luptak, M., Dailey, N., Juretic, M., Rupper, R., Hill, R., Hicken, B., & Bair, B. D. (2010). The Care Coordination Home Telehealth (CCHT) rural demonstration project: A symptom-based approach for serving older veterans in remote geographical settings.

Marks, J., & Augenstein, J. (2019). A Framework for Evaluating the ROI of Telehealth, manatt white paper, 9 November. Available from: https://www.manatt.com/insights/white-papers/2019/a-framework-for-evaluating-the-roi-of-telehealth (accessed 20 January 2020).

Mayor, S. (2020), Covid-19: Researchers launch app to track spread of symptoms in the UK. *British Medical Journal*, (Clinical Research ed.), *368*: m1263.

McCarty, D., & Clancy, C. (2002). Telehealth: Implications for social work practice. *Social Work*, 47(2): 153–161.

McLean, S., Protti, D., & Sheikh, A. (2011). Telehealth for long term conditions. *British Medical Journal*, *342*, 374–378.

Melo, S., & Beck, M. (2014). *Quality management and managerialism in healthcare: A critical historical survey.* London (UK): Palgrave Macmillan.

Nyberg T, Xiong G, Luostarinen J. Connected Health Services Internet, Mobile and Wireless Technologies in Healthcare. In: *Proceedings of 2011 IEEE International Conference on Service Operations, Logistics and Informatics.* 2011 Presented at: SOLI'11; July 10-12, 2011; Beijing, China p. 220–224.

Rashvand, H. F., & Hsiao, K. F. (2018). Integrating telemedicine and telehealth-advancing health at a distance. In: ErenH, WebsterJG, organizers. Telemedicine and Electronic Medicine: Volume 1 (E-Medicine, E-Health, M-Health, Telemedicine, and TelehealthHandbook). Boca Raton Florida:CRC Press; 2015.

Rossimori, A., Mercurio, G., & Verbicaro, R. (2012). Enhanced policies on connected health are essential to achieve accountable social and health systems. *European Journal of ePractice*, *15*(4), 25.

Senni, Michele. "COVID-19 experience in Bergamo, Italy." European heart journal vol. 41,19 (2020): 1783–1784. doi:10.1093/eurheartj/ehaa279 https://www.ncbi.nlm.nih.gov/pmc/articles/PMC7184497/

Shastry, B. S. (2006). Pharmacogenetics and the concept of individualized medicine. *The Pharmacogenomics Journal*, *6*(1), 16–21.

Smith, A. C., Thomas, E., Snoswell, C. L., Haydon, H., Mehrotra, A., Clemensen, J., & Caffery, L. J. (2020). Telehealth for global emergencies: Implications for coronavirus disease 2019 (COVID-19). *Journal of Telemedicine and Telecare*, *26*(5), 309–313.

Sood, S., Mbarika, V., Jugoo, S., Dookhy, R., Doarn, C. R., Prakash, N., & Merrell, R. C. (2007). What is telemedicine? A collection of 104 peer-reviewed perspectives and theoretical underpinnings. *Telemedicine and e-Health*, *13*(5), 573–590.

Steventon, A., Grieve, R., & Newman, S. (2012a). Rapid Response: Why did the Whole Systems Demonstrator report reductions in emergency hospital admissions? Insights from new analyses. Response to: Effect of telehealth on use of secondary care and mortality: Findings from the Whole System Demonstrator cluster randomised trial. *British Medical Journal*, *221*, 15–30.

Syed, Z. (2021). How the department of Veterans Affairs delivered better services during the pandemic. *ourpublicservice.org/blog*, January, 21. Available from: https://ourpublicservice.org/blog/how-the-department-of-veterans-affairs

-used-technology-to-deliver-better-services-during-the-covid-19-pandemic/ (accessed 20 January 2022).

The King's Fund. (2011). Are the whole system demonstrator trial results a watershed moment for the rise of telehealth? Technology and data. Available from: https:// www.kingsfund.org.uk/blog/2011/12/are-whole-system-demonstrator-trial -results-watershed-moment-rise-telehealth (accessed 20 January 2022).

Tuerk, P. W., Fortney, J., Bosworth, H. B., Wakefield, B., Ruggiero, K. J., Acierno, R., & Frueh, B. C. (2010). Toward the development of national telehealth services: The role of Veterans Health Administration and future directions for research. *Telemedicine and e-Health, 16*(1): 115–117.

Vincent B. (2021). How the Veterans Affairs department went digital during the pandemic. *Nextgov.com*, 21 September. Available from: https://www.nextgov .com/cio-briefing/2021/09/how-veterans-affairs-department-went-digital-during -pandemic/185386/ (accessed 20 January 2022).

Whitten, P., & Collins, B. (1997). The diffusion of telemedicine. *Science Communication, 19*(1), 21–40.

Young, L. B., Foster, L., Silander, A., & Wakefield, B. J. (2011). Home telehealth: Patient satisfaction, program functions, and challenges for the care coordinator. *Journal of Gerontological Nursing, 37*(11), 38–46.

Index

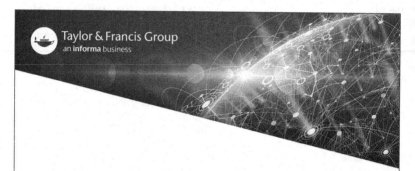

Printed in the United States
by Baker & Taylor Publisher Services